Tools

Help For Women Repairing Their Marriage

Geri Holmes

Copyright © 2020 by Geri Holmes.

All rights reserved. No part of this publication may be reproduced, distributed, or transmitted in any form or by any means, including photocopying, recording, or other electronic or mechanical methods, without the prior written permission of the author, except in the case of brief quotations embodied in critical reviews and certain other noncommercial uses permitted by copyright law.

Printed in the United States of America.

Library of Congress Control Number: 2020919874

ISBN	Paperback	978-1-64803-426-8
	Hardback	978-1-64803-427-5
	eBook	978-1-64803-428-2

Westwood Books Publishing LLC
11416 SW Aventino Drive
Port Saint Lucie, FL 34987

www.westwoodbookspublishing.com

Preface

I am warmed and inspired by all the men and women who take time from their busy lives to engage in counseling. I see their effort and steps of courage as indication that they believe enough in their marriage or partnership to want to hold on to it and make it better. I value their honesty and hold in confidence the sharing of their hearts – both the hurting and vulnerable parts and the angry enraged parts. For that reason any stories or situations described in these chapters are not the details of any one person's story – they are a mixture of stories. *I have taken some literary license in the telling to protect their privacy. And all names and identifiable parts have been changed.*

This book is about communication and expectations in relationships but is specifically directed towards women.

While it is not always the case, from my vantage point, women tend to talk more, read more and certainly appear to think more about making their marriage better. They are the ones who most often initiate counseling. They may come alone and then insist their partners come later. Or they may threaten their spouses out the door by saying, 'you need to get counseling or we are done.'

Most frequently the women I see are fairly convinced their partner is at fault – perhaps he is selfish or does not know how to communicate. Some women complain that their spouse is not in touch with their emotions. Others say they don't listen or they try for a while and then

Geri Holmes

stop trying. They conclude that one (or more) of these reasons is why the marriage is in trouble. Unfortunately, women, myself included, are not always able to see their own blind spots.

Part of the problem is that we women tend to talk about our problems to other women. Ideally this sharing should be a good thing – a kind of community support or sisterhood that assists us in helping each other. However, because we are all women we think much the same: we innocently validate each other's perspectives.

I wrote this book primarily because after facilitating many hours of marriage counseling and having a counseling practice that included at least 50% male clients, I found myself understanding men better and the marital "dance" that often takes place between the sexes. As a result, I found myself saying the same things to numerous women again and again. I finally sat up one day and thought, "Maybe I should write this down!'

Now don't misunderstand me – I am not putting all women in a certain category. It is my belief that each chapter can relate to some women. And no singular woman will fit into every chapter. As the reader, one or two or a few chapters may apply to you while others may not.

However, my experience has shown me that there are enough women that act in certain ways that I feel confident in generalizing.

And for the record, much of what I have shared has been tested out on the women whom I have counseled. Many have told me it was helpful. And of course, that's my goal in writing this book: I want to help women, and help their relationships be better.

It's important though that the Reader comes to this material honestly and humbly and with an open mind. It takes a lot of maturity to see faults in us – it's a lot easier to analyze others.

Tools

I've struggled writing this book because as the author I have not arrived either. At times I have continued to do the very things I've suggested I shouldn't do!

But I am more aware!

And I catch myself quicker.

And that's all I hope you will do too.

In Appreciation

To Doyle
- for thirty-five years of marriage; the seedbed for growth and change

To Marion, Barbara, Sharon and a host of other girlfriends
- for friendship, faithfulness and believing in me

Tools

Help for Women Repairing their Marriage

1. Celebrating Difference

2. Embracing Biology

3. Resigning the Legal Team

4. Decoding Communication

5. Surrendering the Expertise

6. Risking the Truth

7. Laying Down Shields

8. Owning One's Happiness

9. Redefining Commitment

10. Reconnecting with God

1

Celebrating Difference

Although we all agree in principal that we are different from our spouse, and men are different from women, living with that difference can be a challenge. It's a challenge because we believe in the power to change. We believe that if we tell our spouse that something he does annoys us or hurts us, he will at least *try* to change.

But when that annoying behavior continues and there is no change in sight, we can quickly escalate into anger and hostility.

Why is that?

Because many women assume "if you love me you will change." To flip that then, when change doesn't happen, something's wrong with love.

Unfortunately this is not usually the case. Although partners love each other deeply, they actually change very little.

And the fact that they (and we) don't change has nothing to do with love - it is not because we don't love enough. It is not because we are selfish and uncaring.

Geri Holmes

The first tool in strengthening or repairing your marriage is to switch your mindset. We need to look at the irritating behavior differently. We need to look at our spouse "respectfully."

How do we do that?

First, let me define respect.

- To respect someone is to attempt to understand their uniqueness, their own creative strengths and specializations.
- To respect someone is to try, as much as lies within us, to accommodate or make room for those differences to be expressed - in how they approach things, what they value and the way they love.
- To respect is to give up the right to control or demand conformity to my way or to the way I see it.
- To respect is to let go of comparisons and conclusions and judgments about how their partner came to be this way.
- To respect is to honor humanity – that every person has some kinks, disappointing behaviors and failures in life management
- To respect is to honor or celebrate what they offer the relationship, not just tolerate the other person

To summarize, respect is giving honor and value to another's differences

Having differences is good and natural because a marriage consists of two individuals each with their own thoughts, feelings, preferences, tastes, values, desires, goals, behaviors and past history.

And it is these differences that attract us.

One psychologist suggested we are attracted to difference because we intuitively know that our partner has a specialization we don't have. We are truly complimentary.

Tools

And yet it is quite normal that we are frequently angered by the very traits that compliment us.

For example, the introvert is attracted to the extrovert, but afterward becomes angry when the extrovert wants to go out, see people, or check their social media constantly.

The extrovert, on the other hand, is attracted to the introvert who is loyal and steady and caring and kind. But then gets annoyed when their partner prefers to stay home, hold hands and only connect with the family.

As time rolls along, what was fun and exciting is now annoying and disappointing. We fail to see how good they are for us, how their influence balances us, keeps us from our extremes and brings a whole different set of skills to the marriage.

Difference is good. Difference is beneficial. Complimentary differences make the two of us more complete.

How are we different?

1. We are different in personality.

Personality is in our genes; our environment did not shape it.

Even though family members may share habits and behaviors, it may not be a learned behavior. It may be genetic. Studies of twins separated at birth have proven this to be absolutely true.

Personality or temperament studies go back hundreds of years to Hippocrates. He was the first one to identify four different kinds of people. Since then, hundreds of others have done studies on human

3

behavior only to identify similar traits or commonalities. These personality differences have to do with:

- How we approach new people and new things. Some people are very cautious, even suspicious of anyone or anything new. They want to observe or watch others, take their time to know if the person or the "thing" can be trusted. They wait to see if they or it has any benefit to them. Others approach people immediately, enjoy strangers, like socializing and are very trusting and optimistic. They assume the best about people and things.

- How we approach problems or challenges. Some people see a problem as a challenge. They are competitive, driven to prove to themselves it can be done. They are creative thinkers, imaginative and entrepreneurial. They take charge, recruit and assign jobs. They are action-oriented and often impatient. But others approach problems from a "wait and see" perspective. They prefer to follow, to cooperate or allow others to take the lead. They lack the will, confidence and perspective to jump right in. They easily relinquish responsibility.

- How we view change. Some people enjoy change, love variety, hate the "same-old, same-old" They are adventurous and spontaneous. But others resist change. They prefer routines and procedures. They like the familiar, tradition and the status quo. They overwhelm easily if forced to change too much. They get stubborn if pushed into unsolicited changes.

- How we approach rules and authority. Some people are trusting, feel safe and prefer to follow the rules. They are compliant, agreeable and structured. They believe there are "right" ways of doing things and "wrong" ways and knowing what is expected and doing it right is important to them.

Tools

Others see rules as suggestions. They are independent and like doing it their way. They can be independently stubborn, obstinate or self-reliant.

All four personalities handle emotions differently: some are impatient, easily angered and fear failure. Some are impulsive, affectionate and loving but fear rejection. Some are empathetic, compassionate and caring but hate burdening others. Still others are peaceable, steady but don't reveal much emotion at all.

If we understand our own personality and the personality of our partner we can understand better why our approaches to tasks and people are different.

We can also appreciate why our partner does not easily change. Sometimes it is not resistance or their lack of trying. It is very difficult to rewire what's been hardwired in us.

But what happens when we don't accept difference? What does "disrespect" look like?

Probably the first disrespectful thing we do is to blame or shame his family or upbringing for anything and everything that we don't like. (More later on this in chapters to follow)

It is natural for us to compare children to parents and siblings. From the time we are babies we are looking for common genetic characteristics. Many times people have mannerisms that remind us of other family members: the way they stand, use their hands, tastes in foods, or responses to environmental factors. As mentioned already, twin studies indicate that we inherit a lot of characteristics.

So seeing similarities isn't the problem.

Unless we don't like the common trait.

Then it's a dysfunction or a damaged part and we use it as ammunition to shame our partners into change. This is especially shaming if they don't like the trait either.

The unfortunate thing is that even when we see a similar trait in others, or ourselves - one we dislike as much as our partner does - not a lot changes. We just feel less confident, more hesitant and we fear we are unacceptable.

Is that how we want our spouse to feel? Is that how we want to feel? I really don't believe we do.

So let me suggest that we can be more effective in our relationship with our partner if we accept who the person is now, no matter how they came to be this way. We need to love them and respect them at face value.

Many a woman has married their man observing parts of him they didn't like, but marrying them anyway. (Perhaps that's somewhat true of all of us.) The mistake we made was not in marrying an imperfect specimen, but in believing that with just a little kindness and a lot of love we can fix or change what we don't like. As mentioned already, people are quite optimistic about the strength of their love and its positive affect on others. Unfortunately many women become resentful when all that love and sacrifice is not reciprocated.

We are much better off focusing on adapting ourselves and accepting others than changing them.

You may say, well isn't it me changing then?

Not really. Adapting is not the same as changing. It's making accommodations. It's letting go of ideals and living more realistically.

Tools

But hear me out – this does not mean we stop sharing with our partner how their behaviors, attitudes or words affect us, hurt us and annoy us. We will continue to have complaints.

But sharing is one thing, demanding is another.

A few years ago we were renovating our basement. We had gutted it to redo the walls and floors. I had a floor plan in mind that included two bedrooms and a family room. But in the middle of the room were two metal support poles that supported the weight of the house. As we lived in a log home, they were very important for carrying the weight. Those poles were very annoying to me because no matter how many times I tried to change the plans, the support poles were not "fitting." After awhile I gave up and resigned myself to the walls of the rooms aligning themselves to the poles.

As I walked up from the basement that day, having resigned myself to the floor plan, it hit me that my husband was just like that.

He was a metal pole.

I had grumbled and resisted certain things about him most of my life. But clearly he was not "moving."

So what if I accepted him for who he was and I adapted? What if I worked harder at working around him or finding ways to help myself to not be annoyed or expect so much? What if I removed myself from annoying things, looked the other way, or distracted myself more?

A whole list of possibilities emerged. I joined a fitness center to work out. (I had been waiting a long time for him to walk with me.) I found some new hobbies to explore without him and planned a holiday with others because he hated to travel. I set up the spare room as a reading room and office for me to relax in so I didn't have to listen to the TV when it aggravated me.

7

Geri Holmes

'Why was this so difficult before,' I asked myself?

Perhaps because I didn't have respect! I believed as many women do, if he loved me he would change.

Other people's personality traits, kinks and foibles are uncomfortable and irritating. But when we accept the discomfort as part of maintaining a relationship, it definitely gets easier.

2. We are different in habits and learned behaviors

Most of us have habits, non-genetic, learned behaviors. Yes, probably some came from our upbringing although once again how many of our behaviors were genetic is hard to say. You have probably heard it said that it takes three weeks to change a habit. (Actually more recent research suggests it's more like eight weeks.) However, the truth is a habit never changes unless the habit becomes a problem to us. And even then we may struggle to change it.

Consider George. When George walked in the house, he kicked his shoes off at the door. His wife, and everyone else who came in after him tripped on his shoes or were forced to step over them. It was a most annoying habit.

George and Sally talked about the problem in counseling. Sally was so exasperated. (But then again, so was he.) He understood it was a bad habit, he understood it irritated her but he couldn't seem to remember to change it. Of course, she had repeatedly badgered him, shamed him and accused him of being selfish. "You just don't care about anyone but you."

I understood her frustration but his as well. After all, how many times have I tried to change an annoying habit!

8

Tools

One day the couple was out browsing garage sales and saw a small rug with the most appalling colors. Wife said to hubby, "Who on earth would ever buy a thing like that?" Jokingly the husband said, "Well maybe if we had a rug like that I'd remember to move my shoes." She laughed and then paused and said, "You're on!"

They purchased the rug with a smirk. Sure enough from that day forward he moved his shoes. All it took was one look at the ugly rug to remind him. A few months later she said to him, "Do you think we can get rid of the rug now?" He smiled. "Yup," he said. "I think I've got this." And sure enough he had!

What motivated him? Love? Compassion?

Nope. A rug.

Habits are hard to break.

Before we attack our partner we might want to change our approach. A smart women may have many ideas of how to change a habit, however, the change must come from the individual himself. Humor can release a lot of tension and sponsor a creative environment.

On the other hand, some habits won't change and perhaps training the family to look carefully when they walk in the door may not be the end of the world either. When a family loves each other, they learn how to roll their eyes, sigh and move on. They adapt.

Besides, it's almost impossible to figure out what is genetic and what is learned.

What is important is that we communicate. Our partner will come to know us by what we enjoy and by what annoys us. Some things are easy fixes and with gentle reminders changes do happen. Our partner may try to adapt, just as we do, and they may become more sensitive to our reactions. They may apologize more often or even ask for help or reminders.

However, let me restate that if it is a personality trait it probably won't change for long no matter how hard they try. Human beings will naturally fall back into the pattern of behavior that is consistent with how they were hard-wired. A good observation to make is to look at your partner's actions in terms of different environments. For example, does he interrupt others (friends, co-workers, other family members) or just you? Does he forget to do things related to his work, his social engagements or just you?

If there is a consistent pattern in many different environments than its likely personality, not learned behavior. Over time we come to know our spouse and see the kinks in their personality more clearly but we experience them in many different circumstances.

It's so important to continually train ourselves to believe the best about our partner's motivations. It's most probably that he isn't trying to be hurtful, or insensitive or aggravating; he is just this amazingly, unique individual with many different habits and behaviors.

Need a repair in your marriage?

> Look for what annoys you, yes even compliments you, and find a way around it.

OWN it

1. Go back and re-read the "respect" definitions. Ask yourself, "Is this me? Do I respect my partner? Give yourself a score from 0-10. Where could you improve?

2. Take time to make a list of the little and/or big thin
   you about your partner. Let the list develop over a fe

   Consider what you would do differently if you knew absolutely
   the annoying thing would never change? How would you adjust
   yourself to accommodate?

   What support would you offer yourself? Would you hire out? Pick
   up the socks yourself? What? Think about it.

3. Make another list, of the little or big things that you would consider
   his strengths. Refer back to the four personality categories in this
   chapter. What are the things he does for you or other people that
   you/they like about him? (It might be something as obvious as 'not
   making waves.') Do you see him as a compliment or do you take
   those things for granted?

4. If he died, and you lived alone, what would you miss about him?
   Assume you would never remarry – how would you cope without
   him doing the parts he would take with him? Reflect.

2

Embracing Biology

In the first chapter we addressed the issue of respect and difference. Following this theme consider difference in the light of sexuality.

We are different, but not just because of personality. We are different because they are men and we are women. As the chapter title suggests, when we fail to embrace our biology (and our spouse's) troubles abound.

Studies have shown that there are literally hundreds of differences between men and women. One study compared 10,000 genes and found there were 6500 genetic differences between men and women. Another study compared brains and found 100 different functional differences between men and women.

Men and women function differently. For example, women have less stamina than men. Women's blood contains more water and has 20% fewer red cells. Since the red cells supply oxygen to the body cells, women tire more easily and are more prone to faint. Years ago when the working day was increased from 10-12 hours under wartime conditions, accidents increased 150 percent among women but not at all among men. Women have other biological strengths but stamina is not one of them.

Tools

While women are different than men they are not less than men. And neither are men less than women. We each do things differently and because of that each may be suited to doing something better than another. Thankfully, we are not in a competition.

And not only do we do things differently we may feel differently about what we do. This means men may not feel as strongly about the issues women feel strongly about. (I talk in more detail about this in a later chapter)

Frankly I think feminism has done women a disservice. It has led us to believe that we can have it all.

Subsequently we can do it all.

And we can do it just as good as men.

As time has gone by we may have *also* come to believe men can do it (whatever 'it" is) just as good as women.

But I believe both men and women have been given strengths through nature's gifting. I also believe we have corresponding limitations.

The reality is men and women are not, and never will be the same. We can swap clothes and hairstyles but genetics and hormones are not so easy to change.

Meet Paul and Jane.

It's been a long day. A day filled with activities, work, a quick stop at the grocery store, picking up kids and then arriving home late. Stepping through the door Jane's mind is already on many things: the groceries to be put away, the meal to be made, the laundry to go in and the shoes in disarray in the closet she passed on the way in. A pile of laundry waits unfolded in the basket on the living room couch.

Geri Holmes

Jane misses none of this.

Or the shouting, hollering, squabbling and complaining of every kid as she enters the door.

Paul, on the other hand is already at home in front of the TV watching the Sports channel.

After plunking the groceries down, Jane, who is as aware of her spouse, sighs in exasperation and disappointment surrendering yet again to the resentment she carries within. In her exasperated tone she slams down the pot and mutters loudly, "You could have at least got supper started!" The tone immediately puts Paul on the defense. He registers "threat" and mutters something about not knowing what to make. (The truth is he has not even thought about supper because he isn't hungry yet.) He silently gets up and heads outside to his "man cave" to avoid her hostility.

What is wrong with that man, we ask ourselves. How come he is so selfish, and so irresponsible? Does he not care about his hungry kids and his tired wife?

From my work with both men and women over the years, I have discovered this marital dynamic very common. And since over half of my counseling clients are men, I have come to realize some interesting differences.

Men typically respond. Women typically anticipate.

An anticipator (my word, my observations) is someone who considers what someone needs before they need it.

An anticipator observes, studies, and makes mental notes of others so that they can "pre-empt" a need. An anticipator believes without a doubt that this is the true heart of love; that One cannot love without being very aware of needs and preferences of the Ones they love.

14

Tools

Anticipators are not necessarily long-range planners. They are not necessarily detail oriented. (These are personality traits) However they are caretakers, and because of that they want to give the best care possible. To do that, they must think ahead.

Because this is how they function, an anticipator may automatically assume or have an underlying belief that "if you love me, you will anticipate my need as well."

In my experience women are generally anticipators.

As an estrogen-based individual most women do relationships by naturally responding to the needs of their loved ones. Estrogen monitors all the female functions of the body – the production of eggs, the movement of eggs to the uterus, menstruation, pregnancy and long afterward – the care and nurturing of infants. (And much, much, more!) While some men might be good nurturers, women come by it honestly: it is routed in their hormones. (There are many studies to support that human hormones affect human behaviors)

Let me explain further.

When a baby is conceived the Anticipator gets ready for its coming. For nine months they anticipate what their baby needs. (Don't smoke, don't drink, get rest etc.) Once born, they become synced to its movements and its cries. An Anticipator can tell the difference between a hungry cry and an angry cry - and a dozen other little things. When an Anticipator decides to take baby outside, they anticipate the child's needs based on the weather and how long they will be gone. Are there milk, soothers, diapers, wipes and a change of clothing in the bag? This innate sense of intuition, or readiness or nurturance is generally part of who women are. And even women who have never conceived a child generally approach their husbands or family in similar ways.

Geri Holmes

As an Anticipator, most women tend to "nest" with a similar approach. Just as their womb nests, they nest, making their homes ready for living in. They are concerned for hygiene, appearance, health concerns and often beauty and comfort. They anticipate what their family needs and how their home should function. It's true that some women are lousy housekeepers (there could be many environmental factors that have changed us) but for the most part the home still matters.

This anticipatory characteristic is sometimes applied to their careers as well.

Men generally do life differently.

Men tend to be responders.

Unlike his wife, when a husband heads home from work he is not anticipating what to feed the family for supper, what housework is waiting for them, what problems the kids are having at school, or what to do for his wife who is having a birthday (unless he has been forewarned or he has built a routine around one or two or these things.)

What he is thinking about is the traffic and whatever else is happening at the moment. While it is true that some men worry about the future (again, much of this is personality driven), for the most part men are better at being "mindful." (Mindful meaning, living in the moment and focusing on the task at hand.) One speaker, Mark Gungor, suggests men live in "boxes" – they focus on only one thing at a time.

If we embrace the idea that men are responders and not anticipators, then men need triggers in their immediate environment to help them to remember. For example, when they arrive home from work and see the uncut grass they may be reminded to cut it, or when they walk in the house thirsty and see the table set with the glasses, they may be reminded they were supposed to pick up some pop on the way home. Responders live life practically, experientially and immediately.

Tools

Why is this helpful to know?

Hormones affect how we meet each other's needs

Yes hormones affect how we show love.

Without realizing it, many women relate to and show love to their husbands in the same way they love and relate to their child (even before they have one).

They anticipate what their spouse needs.

From the day they begin dating, anticipators make mental notes on what pleases their boyfriend, what their preferences are, and what they like. They know in advance when a birthday is coming and they prepare for it. They know favorite drinks, movies and sporting events.

After marriage they know when the laundry basket is full, they know when the sheets are smelly, when the bathroom is out of toilet paper. Unless they are over-extended in work and career, anticipators effectively show love by meeting needs. This for them is how love is expressed. It's natural for them. It's just normal.

But hear me out now – when the husband doesn't act or think like the Anticipator, the husband is seen as disconnected, calloused and/or insensitive.

If he loved me he would know what I like for my birthday, he would know how tired I am at the end of the day, he would try to "anticipate" what I might need and support me.

"Wait," you may say. "When I was dating my husband, he did seem to remember things I liked or didn't like. Isn't he just taking me for granted now?"

17

Geri Holmes

When a man is dating he has one singular focus (one box): to "win the girl." It is easy to remember when that's all that's on your mind. They are in a state of continual "response."

But when we mate, learning to relate gets complicated.

Life involves more boxes, more events, more people and a very changeable and unpredictable woman.

The truth is women are always changing. Their hormonal cycle affects them. Their environment affects them. The number of relationships they are juggling affects them. Women are not predictable and the amount of effort required for a man to stay on top of all the changes is actually exhausting. It is easier and more natural for a man to respond instead.

One of the reasons why women love romance is that it speaks to the heart of the Anticipator – anticipate what I want right now and surprise me by that knowledge. 'Love me in the way I love you.'

For years I felt unloved because my husband forgot my birthday and/or anniversary. Or if he did remember it was the same old thing – flowers and chocolates. The first time he brought flowers and chocolates I was thrilled. I love both. But when it was the same thing a few years in a row, I interpreted it to mean he was lazy and uncaring enough to think about what I might like. After all, I always knew what he liked!

But then I discovered that if I put sticky notes on his computer, with suggestions of things I might like, he would happily buy me something on the list. Sometimes everything on the list! He was as excited about my birthday as I was, because he knew he would please me – and he wanted to please me.

Because men are responders, they need to be guided – without feeling like they are being controlled. The more consistent the request, and the

Tools

more reliable the routine, the more a man knows how to respond and what to do. I have found women who are very clear in their instructions, who keep routines themselves and have a place for everything and everything in its place have more responsive husbands. Men are much better with doing the same thing, every day, all the time rather than trying to guess what "help me" means when the help is different every day. If "love me" means load the dishes, then let them love you by loading it every day. When "love me" means a different thing every day, or every hour, men become confused and frustrated – especially when they are attacked for not knowing what they are "supposed" to know today.

The truth is responders have their own strengths. The testosterone-based man will protect his wife and family at any cost. Put a problem in front of a Responder and they can be quick to act and to solve problems. (If they believe their problem solving solutions are helpful and appreciated.) When men go to work they feel a great sense of well-being. They work for different reasons than women; by working a man is taking care of, or providing for his woman or family. Work is a practiced, predictable, patterned behavior that gives meaning to life. Of course many women work outside the home too, may even make more money, but in my observation she does it for different reasons.

Hormones affect how we parent

This responder/anticipator difference is very evident when parenting.

Women typically seek to understand the "why." What might Johnny or Susie be feeling or thinking or needing to cause them to act in this way?

Most men on the other hand just respond to the behavior and seldom overthink it. The difference between their approaches is particularly evident when moms are frustrated and exasperated and turn to their husbands for "support." Frequently men hear and respond to the exasperation revealed in the voice of their wife (who has told their kids ten times to do something, only to be ignored). They rise up and shout, "Get that room cleaned. NOW!"

"Honey," the wife chides him. "Stop shouting. You're being so mean. Speak nicer. They're just tired. This empathetic approach, more typical of women is confusing. To most men knowing why someone does something is irrelevant if the problem can be fixed by an action.

In truth he is acting responsibly: protecting his wife and getting results.

Responders, that is men in general, want to succeed, to get it right, to hit the bulls eye every time. They love to meet their wife's needs. But they become discouraged when they don't get it right because of something they didn't anticipate.

If the instructions related to child care are unclear, the standard is too high or if the way they do it isn't good enough it's likely they will procrastinate dealing with the kids. Parenting is a very difficult challenge for dads who are away from home for long periods. Children change, routines change and approaches change. Wanting to help but being unsure of what is expected can be hurtful if his wife seems exasperated that he can't adapt and figure it out for himself.

It is frustrating for women as well. Women complain about men being another child. But patience and understanding without judgment can make it easier on everyone.

This is also true of homecare. Put a list in front of a man that is reasonable and practical, they will do what is on that list unless you keep looking over their shoulder to critique their work. Or, you keep changing the order of things that need to be done. Or you criticize him for not anticipating all the implications of a plan.

Tools

Yes, of course we all bring some baggage from our childhood with us – the mom who nagged us to death, or the dad who was unreasonably angry and demanding. However, understanding the difference between Anticipators and Responders can short-circuit a lot of very negative conclusions as to why we don't all act the same.

Hormones affect the way we look at sex

Overall in marriage counseling men complain more about sex than anything else. Typically, there is just not enough of it! Very few women match their husband's desire, especially after the first year and a half of marriage.

Part of this may be because men are more aroused through visuals than women, and we live in a very sexually provocative culture.

But second to that, sex is an important way for a man to connect to his wife. To him the need for intimacy is primarily met through sex, particularly in the early years of the marriage. As time goes by trust and understanding develop as a part of time spent in healthy interactions together. But sexual connection is still important. When having sex, a man wants his wife to be pleased, to be satisfied and to enjoy it as much as he does. To most men this is the best married life has to offer!

Women connect relationally and conversationally. A pleasant cooperative relationship and a good heart to heart talk is foreplay for sex. But if there is no time or energy for conversation, for understanding and validation, women see sex as prostitution. They feel "used."

The greater the distance in the relationship, the more fights that happen, the more insecure the relationship gets, the more men long for sex. But they may never say anything because they fear sexual rejection more than anything. I have had many men in my office who have not had marital sex for over a year, sometimes two. They want sex

Geri Holmes

as much as they always have but the failure of their wife to initiate communicates a tremendous lack of value.

Why is that?

Women are waiting for men to anticipate all her needs in everyday life. Their failure to anticipate is interpreted as selfishness. Men on the other hand are looking for an immediate response. When women put men off because of all the things they know need to be done before they relax, men hear disinterest.

But sex is important and needs to be worked on. When men have intimate connections such as hugging, kissing or actual sex, their bodies produce a hormone in the brain called oxytocin. This hormone, also produced in the breast of a nursing mother, is the bonding hormone. This hormone is released and creates the "connection." Besides the physical need or pressure built up in a man's body because he has been exposed to provocative images, a man craves that harmony with his wife. A lack of sexuality, especially during stressful times in the marriage may result in feelings of anxiety and panic.

There is much to be said about sacrificial love and "servicing a need." Many women can be too dismissive about a man's request for sex. Unfortunately women may not realize, the more "connected" a man feels, the more likely he will meet his wife's needs for connection in other areas of life.

In this age of pornography it's easy to dismiss its negative affect. A man bonds to the images he sees. Too many images and sex becomes unsatisfactory. His brain, as one researcher suggests, becomes "scrambled." When the brain is scrambled sex becomes unsatisfying. Studies have shown that the most satisfying sex comes from making love to one woman only for a long period of time. He is imprinted and "wired" to that woman.

Tools

Sometimes sex needs a plan.

I had some friends for a few years when we lived in a certain city. They were married without kids but busy career people. I was planning a girls outing with a few of my girlfriends and suggested a Saturday morning breakfast. The half dozen girls in the room all shook their head and laughed.

They said, "If you want Sherry to come it can't be Saturday morning."

"Why not?" I asked.

More giggles.

"It's their sex time" someone said. "Nothing gets in the way of Saturday morning!"

While I rolled my eyes, I remember feeling respect for them. They prioritized and scheduled love. It mattered to them. Of course they connected over breakfast in conversation and enjoying each other's company. It was a morning designated to the two of them.

Yes, in a perfect world men would love for spontaneous sex (a quick response) and would love for their wives to initiate (This would communicate you are choosing to connect with me!) but regular sex is still much better than no sex at all.

A man's sexual urges are the greatest motivators to remind them of his wife's needs. It is often when he desires sex he remembers dishes, housework, being kind and considerate and affection – especially if his wife has been reminding him to do certain tasks regularly. Of course I would hope a man does things his wife needs when he isn't reminded of his sexual urges. But it can be easy for a woman to dismiss her partner's attempts to help because she thinks it's a bribe for sex. As unromantic as it sounds, even if it feels that way, it may be a positive attempt to gain connection.

But remember, because men are not anticipators they need reference points to remember things. The need for sex is a reminder to do loving things - not a bribe or payment for sex.

In summary, what does any of this have to do with repairing a marriage?

I find it sad how many times Anticipators are exasperated by Responders who, "don't think." What they really mean is, you don't think like I do. And they are right!

I am also saddened by the assumption that Responders don't care. "If you really loved me, you would know what I need!" A common Responder come-back would be, "I do love you, so TELL me what you need."

Finally I am saddened by the resistance of women to meet sexual needs. Yes, sometimes men's expectations that it should be "great" and his wife should be "hot" every time are too high. But his desire for you is a compliment to his love for you. It's not just about his ego or his experience – it truly is about turning to his wife for connection.

Can you see how many ways we are different?

Need a repair in your marriage?

> Make peace with your biology and with his.
>
> We are at our strongest when we are the most honest about ourselves. We each bring perspectives and passions to the relationship but trying to remake the other is deadly.

Tools

OWN it

1. Grab a piece of paper or journal and write out quickly all the things that are in your head that you "could be" doing instead of reading this book. Take three minutes. How long is your list?

2. If you want to have some fun, stop your husband in the middle of a TV show or sports game. Throw him a piece of paper and give him 3 minutes to write down everything he could be doing right now instead of watching a game. Warn him though, this is not a "loaded" question – you are not trying to trap him, just having some fun. (Watch for his "deer in the headlights" look, blank stare or argumentativeness: "why are we doing this NOW?") What did you learn about the two of you?

3. Consider "connection" as a significant part of marriage.

    What makes you feel connected to your husband? Is it the same every day, every time? Are you able to give him something definitive, clear or consistent that he could do for you regularly to increase your connection?

    What about what makes him feel connected? Have you ever asked him? This might be a great conversation starter. (But don't be surprised if he brings up the topic of sex.)

Resigning the Legal Team

The bags are packed. The kids are ready. It's time to head out to the farm for Christmas. The plan was to leave after breakfast.

But where is her husband Raphael? He said he was just going to fill the vehicle with gas.

Mikaela is tired of her partner Raphael being late. He has been late for hair appointments, was late for their first family picture appointment (and that was SO embarrassing!) and late for their child's Christmas program. And so it follows when he is late now, she gets hostile.

Mikaela has complained and berated him repeatedly. "You are ALWAYS late," she says. "You NEVER think of anyone else but you!"

Raphael has tried to argue, to defend himself by saying, "No, I am not ALWAYS late." But when Mikaela brings the 'list' forward, reminding him of all those times that he's been late, from the beginning of their relationship until now, he surrenders in defeat. She concludes with emphasis, "Yes, you are ALWAYS late and you NEVER care about me or the kids or the things we need. The only one you care about is YOU!"

At this point Raphael becomes silent. Usually he spins on his heel, storms out the door and slams it behind him. Nothing is resolved. The fight is over – until next time.

And that's how the argument went again…..

So let's take a moment to unpack this.

Could Mikaela, by using a different approach and/or response come out with a better outcome to this problem? Let's take a look.

Over Generalizing

Without intention, by using the words, always and never, Mikaela has hindered her ability to resolve the problem. She has rejected Raphael by using all-or-nothing statements or absolutes.

To use these words is to over generalize and to judge.

The truth is Raphael is sometimes late. He actually has appeared on time for a dozen little things during any given day. He has gotten out of bed in time to dress, eat and get out the door on time for work. He has arrived at job sites on time to do his work and complete it. He was present at the birth of his child and at numerous other family-related activities. He arrived at his wedding and was at the altar before her. There have been dozens of times in the six years of marriage that they have done things together, left the home at the right time and arrived at the right time. Raphael is not always late.

So why does Mikaela use these words? And why does she resist him when he tries to defend himself? What is she really doing?

Mikaela is trying to motivate Raphael to change.

Geri Holmes

Mikaela, like a lawyer in a courtroom, is presenting her evidence. She believes for change to happen Raphael must understand why he is doing this – this "being late" thing - and then he will change it. And he must understand empathetically how it affects her.

But this method, typical to women, does not work.

In fact it provokes a fight.

Why is that?

Because in her over-generalizing and judging, Mikaela is shaming him!

Shaming

When Mikaela lets him have it and in frustration or anger says, "You are always late," he hears contempt. In his mind and through the male filter he hears, "You have a character flaw. A defect. You have something deeply wrong with you that you would have this behavior. You are not enough for me."

"Huh? I didn't say that," Mikaela argues.

But Mikaela might as well have. These are the messages that shame sends.

What is shame?

It's more than guilt – it's that feeling associated with knowing I am not enough; that something is deeply wrong with me.

Guilt, which feels a lot like shame, is a generally helpful feeling because it alerts me to something I did wrong. Because I know what I did wrong, I can admit to the behavior, and change it.

28

Tools

But shame refers to that sinking reality that I am something wrong. I want to hang my head "in shame." I want to cower, regress, hide. Why? Because I don't know why I did it and therefore I feel powerless to change it.

Shame has never motivated anyone to change because when shamed, we raise our shields of self-protection!

Have you ever gained 10 pounds and berated yourself for a day, a week or even a month? "What's the matter with you that you would let this happen? What kind of person are you to have eaten in this way? If you weren't so lazy you would have been working out more and this wouldn't have happened! You have no self-control!"

How did you feel after this tirade of negativity swirling around in your head? Better? More motivated? More confident or ready to change it?

I doubt it.

In fact, the more you shame yourself, the more you believe that you are hopelessly dysfunctional and seriously undisciplined. The more you judge yourself the more you believe that there is some secret thing in you that sabotages your success. The voices of shame render you powerless.

Shame never works to motivate us and it will never work to motivate your man.

When we shame our husbands we remind them that they are helplessness and powerless.

And they will always be because they will never change.

By your words you are actually declaring and reinforcing the idea in his brain that change is impossible.

29

Geri Holmes

But there is a better way!

How much better it would have been if Mikaela would have stuck to the current situation and shared with him that she was annoyed and upset because she had been ready and waiting for awhile.

Unfortunately there is more that Mikaela did to hinder them resolving problems.

Labeling

People frequently use labels. Probably the most common label is "selfish." A man like Raphael who is frequently late is selfish, because in Sarah's mind to be late is to not think of her and the kids. She doesn't realize that she is making his actions personal. She is assuming his actions were intended to hurt her.

Notice how Sarah attaches or associates a message to Raphael's behavior. She judges him. He is not just late, but he is late because he doesn't care about her.

Did he say that? Is that the truth?

Of course it is, she thinks. Why else would he do this to me?

Why else indeed!

What if she thought of each event as a singular event – that one event was not connected to the other? What if she unpacked one event at a time and considered that there was a reason why each and every singular event occurred – and that reason had nothing to do with her personally?

Tools

But when we link all these events together, as a lawyer does, we come to conclusions that are statements of fact.

And we communicate our criticism as a statement of fact.

We do not ask, we tell.

We do not question, we judge.

Labeling and lawyering go hand in hand. When we "lawyer" we pile together a record of wrongs. When we "label" we make statements of fact about another person's character. Finally, "judging" is when we assume negative intentions and motives drove that behavior.

By putting the three together we do great damage and create impossible situations for problems to be resolved.

Nothing will anger a person more than being judged.

So what is a better way?

- We need to realize and recognize other people will disappoint us and fail us, even though they love us and have no negative intentions.
- We need to remind ourselves that relationships will be frustrating at times so we must learn how to manage our feelings without attacking others.
- We need to acknowledge that even though we love others, we disappoint them too.
- And we need to remember that just as we don't always disappoint them, neither do they always disappoint us.

If we really want to see change we have to realize our words have impact.

Geri Holmes

There is a poem by Dorothy Law Nolte entitled, "Children Learn What They Live." She starts by saying,

If children live with criticism, they learn to condemn.
If children live with hostility, they learn to fight.
If children live with fear, they learn to be apprehensive

(The poem continues and is worth the read – see Endnotes for source)

I believe what is true for children is also true for adults. For example, if we say repeatedly, to a friend, "You are so forgetful," is it not likely that when they are with us they may be more nervous and therefore more forgetful?

They believe us. Just as our cellphones store words that we frequently use when texting, and automatically assume we need those words the next time we text, our minds recall frequent accusations and ideas that are said over again and again in conversations.

As women, we want to be believed. We want our words to have impact. We expect others to say what they mean and mean what they say.

So do you truly believe your spouse is altogether, all-the-time selfish?

And is this how you want him to see himself?

I think women underestimate their power of influence. They underestimate their ability to teach.

The best lawyers are very convincing.

They convince their man he is useless, selfish, and cares more for his friends and his work than them. He is inadequate, imbalanced, damaged from childhood experiences, lazy, and insufficient.

Tools

But then, having convinced them, lawyers are surprised when they meet "defensiveness."

But why not? Who wants the label or the judgment?

In chapters to follow we present better ways to influence others. But for now stop and evaluate what communication tools you have been most frequently using.

Some habits can be changed and communication habits are no different. Our job is not to change their habits but to work on ours.

Be accountable. Give him permission to stop you with a hand signal or comment when you use critical words such as 'always' and 'never,' or labeling words. Then correct yourself.

Need a repair in your marriage?

> Use your words to speak truthfully and use them to build rather than destroy.
>
> The truth is that those that perfect the art of lawyering are themselves unhappy people. Why? Because to be a lawyer you have to keep a file. You need to gather evidence. You don't "let things go."
>
> There is a better way.

OWN It.

1. The next time something is really bothering you, imagine your spouse standing or sitting in front of you, turn on your phone and the voice record and let 'er rip! Yes, be as spontaneous and real as possible. Say what you feel like saying. Then review that

Geri Holmes

recording listening for lawyering, labeling or judging. Once you have identified your communication habits, practice a better way. Ask yourself, what behavior would fix the problem. What do I need NOW?

2. On a file card write this phrase: Attack the problem, not the person. For 14 days determine to analyze and evaluate every conflict or argument against this phrase. Do not just evaluate what you thought about him or how you spoke to him, evaluate what you thought about yourself. Look for always and never and shaming statements. How often do you play the phrase, I am not good enough?

Decoding Communication

Every couple has codes.

Like those simple little kicks under the table, or silent glares when in a crowd of people.

Coding has to do with the subtle messages or cues we send out to others hoping they will pick up on them. Once they have interpreted the code we hope and expect them to act appropriately and give us what we need.

Coding may have its place, however, coding can create huge problems in marital communication.

As a starting point, allow me to share this illustration.

Angela is lonely. Her and her husband Jeff have been so busy chauffeuring kids and finishing a renovation in the bathroom that they have hardly had a conversation. They fall into bed together (if he isn't already asleep on the couch) with a grunt of a "good night" and rise the next morning to hit the ground running. Angela hates the disconnection she feels.

So Angela drops a hint. "I'm just not happy right now with our marriage." He stares at her blankly. He is worried already. (She has started many conversations like this. Is she going to leave him this time?) He is silent. His silence is interpreting as disapproval and so she adds to her initial complaint by saying, "We never spend any time together any more. You walk in the door and go straight down stairs and never even greet me anymore." He is still silent, trying to remember when that actually happened. And, where's the question?

She continues with some exasperation creeping into her voice. "Friday you went to help your dad with the seeding and were gone the whole weekend. The kids and I were alone all weekend and had to go to church alone."

Feeling defensive Jeff says, "You know I always do this at this time of year. It's just a few weeks of seeding."

Not getting what she wants, frustrated, she says, "Your family is always more important than me and the kids."

Not knowing what to say, and where to go with this, he says, "Oh for heaven's sake Angela, I'm tired of the same old tirade about my family. We spend just as much time with yours as mine."

With that, in frustration, he rolls over, puts the pillow over his head and emphatically says, "Good night!"

So what did Angela want? And what did Angela get?

Angela wanted more time together so they could connect. She was lonely.

But because of the way she communicated, she failed to get what she needed. The conversation started with "I'm not happy about my marriage right now." and ended with, "Your family is more important than me."

Was she intending to talk about his family? Or was she intending to talk about her lack of connection? Was the thing she wanted related to

Tools

the past – and how he spends his time? Or was the problem a present one – her need to spend more time with him?

According to the research of Dr. John Gottman, eighty percent of the time it's the woman who brings up the complaints in marriage. The research suggests that this is not a problem. But what is the problem, according to his research, is how a woman presents those complaints. It is my experience that many women have poor communication habits.

So let me offer a few better ones.

1. Good Communication is Knowing What You Want and Asking for it.

As a starting point, before we ever bring up a complaint we need to know what we want that will fix it. We may not always get what we want entirely (a win/win solution is the most desirable outcome) but it is impossible to negotiate without a starting point.

Some things are easy fixes: For example, "I'm lonely, could you hold me please." But other things take time to consider.

In fairness, I think Angela knew that her discontent in her marriage was about her loneliness. But her marriage wasn't the issue, her loneliness was. When she introduced her marriage she put him on guard.

"I'm lonely right now, I miss you, the kids miss you," was a great introduction. However she needed to go further with an immediate request such as, "I want to spend more time with you because I miss you. Could we book off Monday night, get a sitter and take a drive?"

Many people are behaviorists, especially men. That means they think in terms of action steps. They respond to problems with immediate solutions. These people can be quite patient in listening but in their brain they are waiting for the bottom line. If the complaint is vague, some kind of "hint dropping," and they can't break the code, they may find ways to salvage their pride by avoiding or shutting down altogether. They may turn over, walk away, get "distracted" either by their phone or the TV or something important they remembered. Some women exasperate their partner because they don't tell them specifically what they want them to do.

Most women love the thrill of being pursued. And most men love pursuing.

But not in communication!

Think of a Jane and George who are divorcing. Jane feels overburdened by the responsibility she is carrying and has carried most of her married life. But in trying to talk to her husband about it she keeps bringing up numerous illustrations of where she felt abandoned by him. He cannot remember any of them – most of them are twenty years old. So George feels helpless. How can he fix it now? What can he do? He sits silently.

She really just wants him to understand her feelings of being overwhelmed and her desire to share responsibility. But because he doesn't seem to understand and show empathy or regret over the responsibility she had to carry, she thinks he doesn't care. And so she keeps giving him all the examples of the past hoping he will understand why they must separate. He is stuck on trying to remember. He remains silent but gets increasingly exasperated. He doesn't know what to say.

When she asked him to leave he was really listening. He was and is feeling the consequences in the here and now. The longer they are apart, the more motivated he is to repair the problem. He loves her and misses her. He wants to change things. But all he hears through his male filter is, "You are a failure. You have always been and you always will be."

Tools

She would have done better to focus on the here and now. What responsibilities should he carry now? Where does she need help? What can he do to change the dynamic?

Quite often women wait too long to confront issues. They drop hints (using code) and keep stockpiling hurt. When they have finally had enough, they unload the pile. Because it has taken so long the hurt feelings are very intense and deep. Women expect men to understand how deeply they feel and validate those feelings.

And frankly they cannot. They can only respond to what you feel now.

I have seen men try to show remorse and empathy. They hug their wife, say they are sorry but it's not accepted because its not enough. May women expect some kind of a response that will show their spouse understands the full weight of years of stockpiling.

Truthfully this is not the man's responsibility. She should have made a big deal after the first offence. Stockpiling is not his issue; it's hers.

If we stay in the here and now, Jane needs to decide which responsibilities she no longer wants to carry and insist he carry some.

And it may be, some day, after he has been given that responsibility, after he experiences the full weight of it all, that he will acknowledge how difficult it must have been for her.

But there is no going backward.

There is only forgiveness and the opportunity for a fresh start.

What's the bottom line he is looking for? Tell me what you want NOW, and I'll tell you if I can do it.

Geri Holmes

2. Good Communication is Listening and Waiting.

Like Mikaela, Angela is good at assuming. She took silence as disapproval, jumped to conclusions about what he was thinking - and kept talking.

Many people have trouble with silence. They want to fill in the blanks about what the other is thinking. They may assume silence means resistance. They may assume silence is the person trying to come up with the "right" answer.

But silence may simply mean 'I am thinking' or 'I am waiting for your bottom line.'

Many people cannot process multiple questions or comments quickly. They are slow processors. In my experience, most of them think in more detail and are more analytical. This "slowness" doesn't make them stupid - just careful: they take awhile to process an incident or answer a question.

When we throw out additional arguments or questions into the silence they may feel like a bag of marbles has been thrown at them. They don't know which marble to grab and deal with so they just shut down – or grab the last one (as Raphael did) missing the whole point of the argument.

If you are married to a slow processor, you may have said, "I just asked you a question. Are you shutting down on me? Or are you thinking?"

Initially it may not be shutting down. It may be recalling, reviewing and trying to remember the circumstances around the event you are bringing up. And by the way, back to lawyering, if you are bringing up past incidents to make your case, they are probably stuck on trying to remember the details around the first example you brought up. When you distract them with the next one, and the next one, they fail to get

40

Tools

your "big point" or your "big conclusion" - because you lost them on the first thing they did wrong twenty years ago. Slow processors deal with one behavior or incident at a time.

Don't interpret silence for a lack of care or concern. Don't assume silence means a lack of commitment.

Yes, its true that some people shut down easily, leave the room and avoid everything at the first sign of conflict. But typically that is because their experience with you or before you has caused them to believe they can never win because they never know what it is they should do.

And that is exasperating!

And yes it is also true that leaving and shutting down can be a protective mechanism. It may be a way of shielding oneself from the boatload of evidence that is coming. Long lectures and rants or "lawyering" has a way of doing that!

So what do we do about the silent response when you are clear and specific about what you need? If the silence bothers you why not ask instead. "Are you thinking about this? Or, are you confused about the question?" Or perhaps, "Do you understand what I need from you?" What are the roadblocks you see?

3. Good Communication Asks Questions and Doesn't Assume Answers

At one point Angela said, "Your family is always more important than me and the kids." (Always?)

Notice, that there were no questions. She didn't ask, "Is the reason you are gone a lot because your family is more important than me and the kids?"

41

Geri Holmes

Many women are skilled at mind reading. No, let me clarify – they think they are. I have had numerous experiences in my counseling office when I have asked the man a question and had the woman answer. And not just about something they experienced together but about what he thought or felt or believed.

Many women are convinced they know their husbands and because men often let them do their thinking and talking for them, they support that notion.

I remember one day my husband came into the house after a day at work, turned immediately to the right passing by the kitchen, went down the hall and disappeared into his office. I was in the kitchen preparing supper. He didn't look at me, greet me or acknowledge me at all. I was hurt and annoyed - like I usually was because this had happened many times before.

I hated it when he did that! It hurt me. I felt ignored and unimportant. (After all, I would never forget to greet him when I came in the door!)

One day after nursing my hurt a few moments, I went down the hall and into his office and said, "Honey, can I ask you something?"

"Sure," he said.

"Am I important to you?"

Silence.

I waited.

He turned his chair around to face me, looking puzzled. "Sure you are important to me."

Tools

I said, "But how come you enter the house, walk right by the kitchen where I am, and don't even say hello - even though you haven't seen me all day?"

Long pause. I waited. Taking my hands in his he looked up into my eyes and said, "I'm sorry. You are very important to me. I just get so focused on getting home to work on this project I forget."

I had a choice at that moment.

I could believe him and accept his explanation. (Which meant I had to change my mind about what I thought or believed about his actions.)

Or, I could argue and insist if he really loved me he wouldn't do that.

I chose to believe him.

Did he change his behavior? Actually no.

But I changed my beliefs, I accepted his good will, and I quit mind reading his intentions. It still annoyed me but not for as long.

I could have kept the fight going. Having spoken to him about how it hurt me, I could have insisted he change. Instead I changed a belief I carried – a belief that imposed a motive on his behavior.

For me the goal of my marriage was not that he keep me happy, but that we be happy together.

4. Good Communicators Lose "the Bitch Tone"

A third thing to note about bringing up complaints is to watch your tone. Jon Gottman, leading researcher in the field of marriage, calls this the "soft start up."

Geri Holmes

Men generally agree that being asked to do something is not usually the problem in their marriage, but being asked with the tone of voice that projects exasperation, anger or sarcasm is a complete turn-off. The commanding, demanding woman is perceived as a threat. The kind, polite and patient woman typically gets more of what she wants.

Most often the man may say, "Quit yelling at me." Or, "Calm down," Or, "Can you just settle down!" This frustrates women because many believe they are being put off or "controlled."

But there is something in the male psyche that reacts to the "edge" in our tone. This is what some men call the "Bitch."

Many men escalate quickly because of the tone. Some get angry and yell back. Some get defensive and dismissive of what you want -which, of course exasperates us further! We escalate by giving them more emotion, more exasperation or anger in our tone.

There is a proverb that says, "A soft answer turns away wrath." I truly believe we all need to take it to heart.

We need to take deep breaths, lower our voice, and speak slower – particularly when we are, like Angela, "exasperated" or "frustrated." We have great power to create the environment for good conversation.

Not fair you say! Why is it always me that changes?!!

Always?

Or ever?

And remember – this book is about you not him.

Tools

5. Good communicators Know What Their Words are intended for

Someone once reported that women use 13,000 more words than men. However, new research suggests this isn't true. They actually use close to the same amount of words but they talk about different things. Women tend to talk about other people while men tend to talk about concrete options or events.

The problem in marriage is not how many words a person uses but whether words have any purpose. A conversation to a man is typically intended to solve a problem or come up with a solution; to a woman, it's just connecting or building a relationship.

Women complain that their husbands are not listening because their men are so quick to offer solutions. Men are actually quite good at listening – they are just listening for different things.

Women often use words as a means to connect. When they vent they are "sharing" - they want to be validated and encouraged.

This can create a big problem – different goals, different expectations.

I mentioned earlier that some people are slow processors. They are usually married to a fast processor. Fast processors actually feel better by talking. They sort out their thoughts and feelings by putting their words "out there." It is important to them to have someone to talk to. They are not looking for someone to fix anything but they are hoping for someone to reflect back like a mirror what the Listener hears them saying. They enjoy it when the listener asks questions, summarizes what they are hearing or challenges a conclusion. Fast processors love a mirror to sort things out. They "externalize."

But many times the Listener, not knowing why their partner is sharing all this stuff, gets lost or overwhelmed.

Geri Holmes

Joan comes home from work and is stressed because of a colleague who is difficult to work with. She finds her husband to vent about the stress.

He, seeing it as a problem, starts suggesting what she might have said differently and done differently. She is offended and exasperated. 'You don't have to fix it,' she says, 'just listen!' His suggestions make it seem like he thinks she's dumb, helpless and can't do her job well.

James on the other hand is annoyed. When she doesn't take his suggestions he feels useless, a failure, and a disappointment in the relationship. ('You should have stayed at work,' he tells himself. After all, he knows what is expected there!)

As exasperated as she may be at his fixing, the truth is she does want a fix. It's not a fix of her work problem but a fix for her emotional distress. She is reaching out hoping for a certain behavior from her man. What is that behavior?

Show me sympathy. Perhaps, hold me. Reassure me. Comfort me. Remind me you are proud of me for hanging in there, remind me I have what it takes or sooth me because I'm anxious.

It would be so much better if Joan would begin her conversation with a clearly stated behavioral request such as, "I'm feeling stressed about what happened today. I want to download what happened. But I don't need anything from you other than to listen, to hug me and to tell me I will be okay. I just need to sort things out. Will you do that?"

Sound fair? Understand however, this request assumes the person listening will have a strong ability to handle emotions – either his or hers. Not all men can listen to an emotionally charged woman and stay cool and detached. This is particularly true if their wife is distressed. If they love her and someone is hurting her in any way, intentional or otherwise, they may naturally want to attack the perpetrator or rescue her.

46

Tools

One woman complained that her husband was addicted to his phone – checking messages, looking at social media or surfing the net. But when we talked about it together, we discovered he was overwhelmed by the long litany of words and lectures. His phone became an escape for him – something simple he could manage and respond to.

Venting is not wrong but most men would prefer a lot less of it. Why? Because words have impact!

I love to vent, and I did lots of it on my husband. I shared my hurts and my feelings. Because I tend to overthink things, I also shared imagined hurts, and read the minds of my offensive co-workers, judging them by deciding about their intentions. Because I can be very persuasive I convinced my husband of how bad those people were. He believed me. But then, having vented I felt better, went back to my work or relationships, forgave them quickly and moved on.

He was confused. He couldn't understand how I could like them, and even socialize with them in the future after what they did to me. He withdrew from them, resented the fact that I should want him to come with me at the next event where those people were present. I chided him, and tried to shame him for holding things against them. Let it go, I said. I was disappointed that he would withdraw.

Clearly, I needed to take responsibility for the impact of my words. Gossip is gossip no matter who is listening. Our spouses cannot be "objective," distant, unfeeling robots that have no reactions of their own.

Yes, we all need some safe place to work through our problems. Ideally we want our spouses to be that place. However we may need alternatives such as having other friends who are confidential and good listeners. We may need to use journaling, or voice memos to record our diatribes. We may need to pray or meditate or walk it off while "pounding the pavement."

Geri Holmes

I am not suggesting we stop sharing but if we are going to vent we need to be sure to take responsibility for what the outcome might be – even in spousal relationships.

Overall I think we need to condense what we say.

Do you remember the communication tool called KISS? – Keep it simple sweetie. This is a great tool when it comes to communicating complaints to a man.

So how do we do that? Let me summarize this chapter:

1. Think it out before you speak. What is my complaint? (What action, or attitude do I want to complain about?)

2. What is the solution for this complaint? (What action or behavior could I suggest that may fix the problem?) Be open for his ideas too.

3. Stay in the present (What do you want him to do NOW about this?)

4. Be patient, as we hope he will be with you. Recognize it takes time to change or adapt a new pattern of behavior. Appreciate and encourage his attempts to change.

5. Before you bring up every little thing, ask, Is it worth the fight? Are you just annoyed or irritable? Is this a mountain you want to die on? Are you creating a contentious home with constant complaining? (It's very draining to live with constant negativity.)

There are no bad guys and good guys when it comes to communication. It is an on-going learning curve. But we improve our communications when we are willing to acknowledge our own poor habits.

Need a repair in your marriage?

> Accept yourself complete with thoughts, opinions, and desires. Don't apologize for who you are or what you need. But then think it through so that when you ask for what you need, you can ask clearly and with confidence.

OWN it.

Rate yourself in the following areas out of 10. 0 is not at all, 10 is quite frequently. How often do you do these things?

1. Being general, gathering evidence, lawyering?

2. Telling him what he is thinking (you just think…) or telling him why he is doing what he is doing?

3. Leaving a complaint hanging without giving a solution or "fix?"

4. Raising your voice, or sounding "edgy" or impatient when making a complaint?

5. Venting?

Based on your 5 scores, pick the one you most need to work on for the next 30 days. Here are the corresponding goals that you could focus on.

If #1 then, be more specific and not general
If #2 then, ask questions, don't assume his thoughts or "read his mind"
If #3 then, ask for an action or offer a solution
If #4 then, deliver your requests without exasperated sighs and sharp and impatient tones of voice
If #5 then, keep venting to a minimum.

5

Surrendering the Expertise

We live in a very "psychological age." What I mean by that is we have come to understand that our parenting, or early childhood experiences have impact on our lives and may shape who we are. With that thinking comes the idea that we are moldable.

I have already mentioned the need for respect in marriage: for us to acknowledge our partner is different from us. However, even if we accept personality differences in each other, a common thought in society is that the annoying parts are probably damaged parts. For example, extraversion soon becomes, "You're addicted to your friends." And that ability to support and follow others really is, "You are so out of touch with yourself, you never know what you like or dislike."

Playing the Shrink

Once we decide that the annoying parts are damaged parts we take the Expert chair - in this case the Shrink chair. You know what I mean... we become the psychologist, the in-house counselor. We diagnose our spouse and make it clear that he has "baggage" and it needs to be changed.

Tools

I am not suggesting our motives are wrong or evil in some way. We always want what's best for the people we love and care about it. We love deeply and throw so much of our energy in doing our job well. Women read stuff, surf the Internet, watch u-tube videos and TV shows hoping to gain insights into the things that worry them and bother them. We continuously want to improve our relationships.

And what a wonderful thing it is to get insight about ourselves: to realize where we have wrong beliefs and wrong ideas about things. What a wonderful thing to get counseling and improve our self-worth and identify our gifts, to understand our wounds and the habits of self-protection we have developed. This is all good.

But it is not a wonderful thing when we use our revelations to categorize and analyze our spouse – to treat him like a project and insist he "gets some help." It is particularly not wonderful when we tell him he has "issues" and so does most of his family. We start reminding him of his messed-up siblings, or his alcoholic father, or his co-dependent mother (or any number of new diagnoses that are floating around.) It concerns and bothers me how many women think their husband has "depression", is "bi-polar," "narcissistic" or is a "workaholic." Of course there are people who have these conditions. But my concern is we throw these labels out so lightly, so freely and our husbands are listening.

It is not a woman's job to diagnose her man.

Like shame, these constant "diagnoses" seldom motivate a man to get help. They reinforce the notion that they don't have what it takes to be a good husband, and they are really undeserving of love.

Is there ever a time to talk to a partner about things so that the relationship can grow? Yes, of course. And it's always good to speak about how behaviors affect you and how actions hurt you. Just be careful when you do that you do not overanalyze and hypothesize.

Geri Holmes

The following story illustrates how incorrect our analysis can be.

Janice had the look of desperation. Her partner of eight years (second relationship) worked long hours and often weekends. When he was home he was good with her kids and helpful. But he hadn't wanted sex for a very long time. She felt rejected and missed his touch and the intimacy it brought.

I tried suggesting they have a designated time each day to connect in conversation, perhaps slowing life down, but when they tried that he was too restless, wouldn't look at her and kept checking his cell phone. It ended in a huge blowout.

During the blowout she brought up the fact he had been abused. She told him he had intimacy issues and needed help. She told him he wasn't capable of having healthy relationships and brought up his past breakups.

Pete's head hung down as she shared this in a marriage counseling session. He worried a lot about whether being abused made him different. I knew her words struck fear in his heart. But Peter really loved his wife and wanted to change.

So Peter agreed to do some individual counseling. It was easy to assume, like his wife did, the problem was the child abuse.

As the counselor explored his relationship he explained his disinterest in spousal sex and his inability to feel attracted to her. He had a long-standing habit of viewing pornography that had escalated over the years. This was a big problem in his life.

As he worked on the addiction with the counselor his desire for his wife began to return. When he finally confessed the problem to his wife, she was surprised.

She had entirely misdiagnosed the issue.

Tools

Later when she spoke alone with the counselor she said, "Well why didn't he just tell me the truth."

Sounds reasonable. So why didn't he?

First, he felt guilty. And every time he was with her in an intimate way his guilt surfaced.

Second, and more importantly he felt hopeless. She had told him more than once in other fights – his abuse was the problem. It was the problem for most everything in the marriage.

And so he thought, "What if she was right? What if he was forever and always not enough for her?" And if he already was unacceptable, how would she ever accept him when she knew what he was struggling with!

The saying goes, "a little knowledge is a dangerous thing."

And that is true of counseling as well.

I speak from experience when I speak of sitting in the shrink chair. I have always been an avid reader and learner and I dropped lots of books onto my husband's lap, re-read lots of chapters to him, and dragged him to counselors. (This was long before I became a counselor myself.) The truth is before we ever got to the appointment I had already concluded and communicated directly and indirectly that he was the problem in our marriage. No wonder he, like most men, didn't want to go. Although he sarcastically scoffed me, he fearfully believed me.

It takes a lot of courage to go to a counselor just to have it confirmed that we are damaged and broken. It's the same kind of angst we feel when we make an appointment with a doctor, convinced we about to hear the bad news that we have cancer or some other fatal disease.

53

Geri Holmes

I'm not saying women should bury their head in the sand and never read any books or watch any podcasts. In fact it's great when we grow! And we can share what we've learned, how we've grown and anything we've gained along the way as a matter of conversation and connection.

But we must be careful not to manipulate with information. Most men can tell when what is being shared is really about them, not us.

The best way to promote any product is to use it ourselves. The best way to promote counseling is to live out the changes in our own lives. As the saying goes, "actions speak louder than words."

If we really think our husband has "issues" then he needs encouragement and hope, not sarcasm or shaming to motivate him. The more we tell him what's wrong with him the less confidence he feels in his ability to bring about change.

But what's with all the psychoanalysis? Perhaps, if we are honest, we are afraid.

In Janice's situation, the behavior she needed was sex. But her real fear was that he was having an affair. She worried she wasn't attractive to him anymore. Her fear drove her behavior. She started psychoanalyzing to take the focus off of her anxiety.

Playing the Tutor

A second place where we play the Expert is in deciding how things should be done.

In fairness to women I think both sexes can do this.

Tools

Life is like a Sandbox

Imagine two children, Sally and Samuel playing in their own respective sandboxes. They went to sandbox Camp because they are friends and they thought it would be fun to go together.

Let's assume both have played in sandboxes before. Sally always built a castle in hers. Samuel always built tunnels and highways and construction sites (good for demolition). But they didn't know that when they went to Camp.

Both of them expected the other to play with them doing what they enjoyed. Sally thought Samuel would help her in castle building. Samuel thought Sally would get excited about road building and clap and cheer when the 'explosions' happened.

They each have sand toys provided for them but they are different. And they are using their toys in their own way.

When they arrived at camp they immediately went to the sandboxes, each working side by side. Time went by. Sally looked over at Samuel and noticed there was no castle emerging. What's wrong, she wondered. She peeks over. There are hills of sand and deep holes.

Surprised and annoyed she thinks, "Hey that's not how you use a sandbox." What's wrong with him that he doesn't play right? Must be because he's never been to camp before!

So she starts hollering over. "Hey, you're not doing this right."

He ignores her. He knows he's doing it right.

She persists and says again, "No, that's not the way it's done. Would you like some help?" (Sally's a nice girl.)

55

Geri Holmes

He ignores her again. He is getting ready to orchestrate a large crash on his demolition site.

And he does.

Sand goes flying everywhere.

Sally hollers, "Hey I told you you're doing that wrong. Look, you're getting sand everywhere. What's your problem?? You need help!"

He stops. He notices the sand on the floor. He sees her angry and frustrated face. He's a little confused.

Is he bad? Samuel likes girls and he likes Sally. But she is unhappy with him so maybe he's done something wrong.

His hesitation is an invitation for Sally to get into his sandbox. "Here, let me show you," she says. "This is a better way to play."

And slowly Sally takes over his sandbox. She's happy, she has someone to share a sandbox with.

He is watchful. It's not much fun and its awkward. He liked the way he did his sandbox. But now he doubts himself: maybe the way he plays is wrong? Is it? Sally seems to think so. She keeps saying, "I know you've never been to camp before, but that's okay." And then, "I know you have never had anyone teach you about sandboxes."

But that doesn't feel okay. It sort of makes him feel like something's wrong with him.

After a while he starts to feel controlled. He is getting resentful. He thinks, "Who made the "sandbox" rules? Who says it has to be for castle making?"

56

Tools

He gets angry. They fight. He shouts at her, "Get out of my sandbox."

They play alone now. Samuel finds other friends at camp who like tunnels and demolitions. Sally finds friends who get it – they know sandboxes are for castle building.

And this is what people do with their marriage. They have expectations. They have rules. And without realizing it they start controlling each other's sandboxes. Or they start shaming or analyzing their partner for being different from them and having a different approach to life.

"You're just like your mother," we say, knowing, we had conflict with our mother.

"You never had any siblings," we say, "that's why you communicate so badly."

There's something wrong with you if you play with sand a different way.

But just as our personalities are different, our history is different. And our approach to our work will be different. Because we approach things differently there will be misunderstandings. These misunderstandings can be sorted out if we do not interpret what is happening incorrectly. We need curiosity. We need to ask, "Tell me why you approached it that way?" Or, "Tell me what you like about the way you play with sand?"

Once again, here is an example.

May wants her husband to spend more time with the kids. So in her mind, she has envisioned the family going to the park for a picnic and kicking a ball around. She drops a hint during the week something like, "Hey, I thought we could do something on Saturday together." Husband Gary nods.

Geri Holmes

Saturday morning comes around and Gary is heading out the door when she says, "Where are you going?" Gary says, "Just out to the shop to work on the quads. Jim's coming over."

"I thought we were going to spend some time with the kids today? Go on a picnic or something," she replies.

"Go on a picnic? Nah, I want to get these quads working before the summer's gone."

"But why can't you do that on Sunday, or next week?"

"I told Jim to come over today," he says.

"Why does he always have to come over? You spend way too much time with him. I think he matters more to you than the kids."

"Look, I want to get the quads done so Michael and Mitch (his kids) and I can take them out next weekend."

"Yeah but I wanted to have a picnic today. The weather is nice for change."

"Well go have one – go without me, or let's go later."

"No, it gets too cold in the evening. Can't you do that later?"

Frustrated she stands and broods. Her anger rises. She blurts out. "You know what, I think you're just afraid of having a real conversation with the kids. You're just like the rest of your family. All you know to do is quad and sled."

Exasperated he leaves, shutting the door with a bang behind him. He feels defeated and angry. His plan to take Michael and Mitch out has lost some of its joy.

How is this like the sandbox? How is she like a Tutor?

58

Tools

She wanted her plan. He wanted his. When he doesn't embrace her plan she starts managing his time and assuming the worst about his intentions. Forgetting to keep the problem the focus (time with kids and family together) she jumps to anger. (There's the sandbox.)

Finally she analyzes and judges him. (There's the Tutor) Why? Because in her mind picnicking is the right way to spend time with the kids. Her way of thinking, which is so natural for her, it is the right way to think.

Did you know that your sense of what's "right" might not always be right for everyone else. (Just try doing a renovation project together!)

What's interesting is Gary wanted time together too but he had a different plan. He actually did think about his kids when he thought about getting the quads going. Is his plan better or worse than hers? It's different. It's just not what she pictured. And its not what he communicated.

We could blame Gary for not explaining and of course he carries part of the responsibility for not communicating his intentions. But in my experience women's judgments rather than questions bring a halt to communication.

More importantly, and in keeping with the theme of this chapter, what if she stopped herself from judging her husband when he planned things a different way? What if she showed appreciation for getting the quads going, for wanting to do stuff with the kids? And then said, "So I like your plan but I had one too. And I'm feeling disappointed because we won't have time for a picnic. When can we go?"

Perhaps the next day, or perhaps next week the quading could be combined with the picnic. Who knows?!

Geri Holmes

We all get disappointed, and we all have different plans and expectations. The caution is to be careful not to take over another person's life just to get things our way.

So let's wrap this up.

Are we disappointed in one another? Sure. And no matter how much we try to accept another we are frequently frustrated and angered by the different responses to a common problem. It's okay we are disappointed. But we need to learn how to handle disappointment without assuming something's wrong with the person who disappointed us.

It may take a few minutes to regroup, to adjust mindsets, to accommodate. Of course it's very helpful to be self-aware so we can be honest with others and ourselves when we are disappointed and frustrated. Many times we act automatically and react defensively if we are not aware.

The hard part of living with someone is communicating our plans without controlling their response, and without manipulating, shaming or controlling their actions.

The other hard part of living with someone is realizing that we may always have different ways of getting the same things – or if not exactly the same thing, a variation of it.

For a few years of my life I became interested in natural treatments using vitamin and herbal therapies. Every ailment had a natural cure. Before long I had quite a wide assortment of bottles on my countertop. That is until a friend of mine was hospitalized for a severe health issue. It turned out a vitamin supplement she was taking was creating havoc in her body. I became aware that even natural things may have serious implications. At that point I decided to engage a Naturopath. I relied on him to diagnose and treat.

In the same way, in this age of knowledge with the Internet so accessible to us, it is very easy for us to play the expert. We become self-help gurus. We find "reasons" why someone is different than us and then throw our thoughts and energies into manipulating change. As I mentioned in the preface, women have women who tend to think alike and support each other's thinking.

So the big questions are, should we ever offer advise on better ways of doing things? Is it wrong to suggest our partner may gain something from counseling or a book, or podcast? Is it wrong to suggest they use a different approach or engage the kids in a different manner?

No of course not. But here is the key: Ask first! Honey, I like your idea but would you like me to suggest a different way? Honey, would you like to hear my thoughts on this? Honey, I would approach this different – would you like to hear how I would do it?

This is what makes a man different from a child. We don't ask our kids permission to instruct and teach and advise. But we must ask our men!

Be forewarned that this switch of approach may take some adjustment on his part. If he is used to you having all the answers, criticizing his approaches, or judging him incompetent (damaged or broken), he may be suspicious about your questions. But be sincere.

And be willing to accept his No! If he makes a mistake, he will learn by them – just as we do.

Want to repair your marriage?

> Ask more questions. Don't assume or judge motivations. Be responsible for your own journey and let him be responsible for his.

Geri Holmes

OWN it.

1. In your journal list the characteristics, habits or qualities you dislike in your husband. Ask yourself these questions:

   Who do you attribute these characteristics to, or what do you blame them on?

   What if your assessment is wrong? What if they are simply genetic or habit driven? What would change in your approach or your emotional response to these behaviors?

2. Think about the last few arguments you had with your spouse. Take a moment to view the situation as a sandbox. What approach did your husband use or suggest? What approach did you? Who's right and why do you think so? Or what if there is no "right" – just different? How may you have handled it differently?

6

Risking the Truth

Women are really great at love. I mean that sincerely. We feel love deeply. We give, we serve. We sacrifice.

But many women carry a lot of romantic notions. They love to imagine, idealize, pretend and create scenarios of the princess life, the prince-charming rescue, the castle and the song of love that swings us on the dance floor. They love to be pursued, and cherished.

I meet women who are really strong, some physically active, even weightlifters. I meet other women who are really tough because they have survived hardships and hurt and had to be brave and courageous. And then there are women who just project strength because its what the culture has told them they should be.

And yet lurking beneath those capable strong exteriors are women who frequently feel weak and long to be able to lean on a partner when they feel vulnerable.

When I allude to this in a session, usually to help a husband see how much their wife really needs them, these brave women will often tear up, look fragile and cry. The men are often surprised by the women's behavior because this is NOT what women project or communicate.

Geri Holmes

And it reveals something about what many women do. They don't life authentically!

Many women lie in ways that are not obvious. They say one thing but mean another. They drop hints but when men ask them directly what they need (because one or two of those men actually pick up on something) they say the opposite of what they mean.

Is it an intentional lie? Probably not - it's usually just an insecure pattern of relating.

Janett is really tired. It's her period week. She really wants a day to chill: to just stay in her room and watch movies for a few hours. She doesn't want to have to clean, cook or tidy. But its Saturday and Monday is coming. And the kids are home and need to be fed.

Janett's husband Peter has just finished his ten-day stint of working twelve-hour days. He has his five days off starting today. He's tired too. But he's not thinking of staying in bed: He's been dreaming of a getting his bike out and hitting the outback. It'll be great. Maybe take his friend Joe along for one day on this weekend.

He comes in from the garage to find Janett shuffling around in her pj's and the kids randomly arranged with cell phones in hand. He grabs a coffee and a couple of pieces of toast, and chats pleasantly about his plans while she digs out the cereal and milk for the kids. Janett's kind of quiet.

He doesn't notice it at first, but then, "Hmmm," he thinks, "something's up. She's usually pretty chatty."

"Everything okay Hon?" he asks. "Fine," she says. "You sure", he says. She ventures in, "Yeah, I guess. I was kind of hoping you'd help me out a bit. I'm not feeling the best."

Tools

Silence. (He's thinking). Feeling disappointed he feels caught. He loves his wife and kids, no doubt about it. But he's really not sure what "help me around here" means. So he's waiting for more information. She sighs. He asks, "So what do you want help with?"

(He is committed to his wife and committed to helping. But of course, he's hoping he can get whatever "it" is done quickly and still get going.)

She picks up on his silence. He isn't enthusiastic.

She's disappointed. She wants that feeling of being cherished, that gallant, upbeat, "Anything for you babe," response. But that's so childish, she thinks. So she says with a sigh. "It's okay. Never mind. Just go"

"Really? Are you sure?" He doesn't leave right away. He waits. He needs to know what is expected, what is wanted. He is the responder.

But she says again, "No, no its okay. I'll be fine. There's nothing much going on today anyway."

Relieved and happy he pecks her on the cheek and off he goes, coffee in hand, excitedly focused on his biking adventure.

Six hours later, Janett is fuming. It's past supper. He isn't home. He didn't respond to her text or call to check up on her. He's off having his good time and he doesn't give a rip about her. He could have at least come home early!

"I told him I wasn't feeling great," she mutters to herself. Her rant continues in her head…. She works and slaves and accommodates him all the time. Why is it, when it's her turn, he's got no time! What about all the times she changed her plans to suit him? What about all the sacrifices she has made chauffeuring kids while he plays rec hockey?!! And now he can't even call to let her know where he is. He could be dead somewhere.

Geri Holmes

Need I go on? Can you hear it? I can. I've been there. Resentful. Tired. Mad.

Its 8:00 p.m. before he comes in the door, tired but bouncy. He has conquered the hill, forged the deep muddy depths and come out dirtied but not beaten. She's on the couch in a semi-state of consciousness but she's awake enough to ignore his hello, to act disinterested and to look like a dark cloud.

He sees it but he doesn't get it. He has no clue. Her silence deflates him. He was excited to get home to her. He wants to share his great day with the woman he loves. He is confused. And by the way, his cell phone is dead.

You see Peter believed her.

When he offered to help she didn't say. "Good. I want you home today. I need you today. I would like to veg in my room today so I really need you to take over the kids, make lunch, tidy the kitchen and take the kids out somewhere." No. That's not what she said. She thought about this list but she didn't say it. What she DID say, was, "No, no its okay. I'll be fine. There's nothing much going on today anyway."

And he, being a man who takes words at face value and acts and responds according to requests, believes her. She is fine. She is okay. And she says he can go.

Once again, in counseling, I have said in my own puzzled voice, "But, you TOLD HIM he could go." And she looks at me, mad. Why?

Because she expects me to know, to get it, to understand - I'm a woman and this is the game we play.

And there are unspoken RULES!

Tools

Rule #1: It's an act. Don't believe what women say.

All male players MUST know what women really want and because they are compelled by love and romance, driven by some phenomenal male instinct, do the very thing we REALLY want (without us telling them.)

You see in this game, we want to be fought for. We want to be pursued. We are coy, shy and not obvious.

We don't want to be believed!

Rule #2: Read my mind. Know what I need without me telling you.

And to a man, this rule is crazy making. Should I believe what she says, when she says "Okay go?" Or should I not? Should I enjoy myself if I go? Or should I go and be ready to be punished when I get home?

Women, you need to know, although some comedians have picked up on it, most men don't like this game!

I wonder where this game began. Who wrote the rules for it? It stinks and it's confusing and it's exasperating. So why do women play it?

I think I know.

We lack confidence in ourselves – and lack the ability to legitimize our own needs. We fail to give ourselves credibility. We are afraid. Afraid of being the thing we are so quick to label others with – we are afraid of being selfish, demanding, "difficult," a nag or some other horrible thing.

Perhaps we feel guilty for having this need. We don't want to be "needy."

Geri Holmes

Perhaps we don't want to express it especially when we recognize that our hardworking husband also needs a break and fun, and we don't want to be "selfish."

Or perhaps this is our definition of strength, and women must be strong!

Women are wonderful at lovingly and unselfishly caring for others. But we have little regard or care for ourselves.

We are insecure in our acceptance of who we are TODAY. We want to be more than we are – some perfect version of ourselves, but we are not. We want to be loved without having needs. We want the superior action of giving without the humbling grace of receiving. We deny our humanity.

We second guess, disqualify, and surrender ourselves into nothingness and wait, no EXPECT him to metaphorically "dig around and find us buried deep within ourselves, and pull us into the light." We place our value in his hands, and wait for him to give us our true value back.

But it all goes amuck. We feel devalued - because he failed to get his hands dirty in our stuff. We feel like the losers. We resent him as a winner. We tell ourselves, he always gets what he wants. (Although that's not likely always true.) But we enable it.

But we seldom ask assertively for what we need.

It's hard for women to admit that it might be their problem that prevents them from getting what they need.

They are equals in this relationship. Their needs are of equal value – not more, not less. Equal. But to grab onto my equality means to know myself, know my needs and validate them.

It's a false reality, a lie of sorts, that says I can give, I can sacrifice, and I don't need anything, ever.

It's also a false reality that my husband will know those needs I deny.

Rule #3 – If I love you enough you will love me in return.

I have a story to share with you, an analogy of sorts.

Below you will see a box, which represents a room. It is the main room of your house. Notice that in that box are two circles. Circle A represents you. Circle B represents your partner. Notice that they are the same size and take up the same amount of space because in this story they have the same value. (And of course, you do!)

You will notice that there are doors around this room – doors to other things you need: the bathroom, the kitchen, the bedroom, the garage.

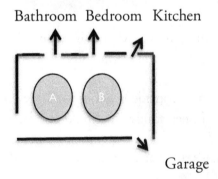

Now let's imagine a scenario. Wife (A) is a working woman. She has a stressful job. One day because her child was sick the night before, she slept so soundly that she failed to hear her alarm. She leaves for work in a frantic hurry without her lunch. She intends to pick up something but it is one of those days where the hectic pace doesn't make room for a lunch break. By five o'clock she is starving. Low blood sugar makes her feel dragged out.

Geri Holmes

She walks in the door and Husband (B) is there already (he works a really early shift) and is sitting in his comfy cozy chair. He has the TV on the sports channel (one of his favorites) and is thoroughly lost in the program. Wife A really, really needs to get to the kitchen for something to eat.

But we have a problem.

Look carefully. What is it?

If you look carefully you would notice the size of this room. Notice the position of B. If A needs to get to kitchen how's she going to manage it? What must she do?

Did you answer – get by him?
Did you answer – ask him to move?

If you said, get by him, how exactly will you do that? Make yourself smaller? Squish, squash, suck it in? How small do you have to make yourself to get by?

If you said, ask him to move, what if he won't? What if he says, 'Just wait a minute. Can't you see I'm watching my show?'

Now perhaps you are confident enough to say, "I'm hungry dear. I didn't have lunch. I need food fast! Could you let me by?"

And he says, "What's the matter with you? Why didn't you take lunch?" (You explain)

"You're so disorganized," he comments with disgust. "I've been telling you for months to make lunches the night before. Besides, why do you trust that phone of yours? You never hear it when it rings. You know if you would deal with these things you wouldn't be in this mess."

70

Tools

So you hesitate. You plunk yourself in your chair quivery and shaken from lack of food.

Why?

Maybe you are feeling ashamed of yourself? Maybe his accusations shut you down and in the moment make you feel guilty and inadequate. Maybe you agree with him. He is right.

But how does any of this help you NOW? No matter what the reason is for your current state, your need is now.

What should you do?

What do you typically do?

Stay there? Wait it out? Hope he has to use the washroom so he will get up and leave his chair and you can get to the kitchen? Or just sit down in silence?

And what about tomorrow when it's all over and you've finally gotten your food before nearly collapsing on the floor – are you angry, bitter, resentful?

So let's unpack this analogy a bit. Do you realize what just happened?

Because you didn't want to make a fuss, you just minimized your need. Because you didn't believe your needs were valid you quietly but resentfully gave it up. In doing so you taught him something – something about you and your needs.

You taught him that if he blames you and guilts you, you will surrender space in this relationship.

71

By sitting on the chair rather than holding your ground kindly but firmly and expecting him to accommodate you, you made yourself (and your needs) smaller. You opened up space for him. And consciously, or subconsciously, you taught him to devalue you.

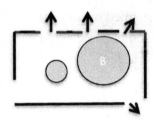

So what about the next day? You're on your way home when you get a text from Honey. "Hey," he says, "could you stop at the store and pick up some batteries for the remote?"

You're tired, dragged out and just want to get home. "No," your mind says. But then the game kicks in. Deny, suppress, serve, sacrifice because if you don't...... If you don't, what?

He'll punish you, shame you, give you the silent treatment?

We allow our fears to determine the level of our guilt because there is that unspoken rule #3 in this game: If I love you enough you will love me in return.

Really? Is love earned?? Is your right to be loved based on positive report cards, good performance, keeping him "happy?"

Or are you worthy of love? Are you worthy of respect?

Can you kindly but firmly say, "Sorry Honey, can't stop tonight. Just not feeling it right now! Perhaps you can go get them when I get home, or I'll make a plan to get them tomorrow."

Because what will happen if we keep playing this game? What do you think it will look like over the space of weeks, months, or years?

Will he acknowledge the many times you gave into him, when you surrendered your need so as not to disrupt his? Will he love you more because he realizes what a loving, caring woman you are to wait on him, and let him have his comfort?

Sad to say, that's not typically what happens. This is.

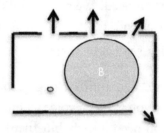

Wife A is a dot. She believes she has lost herself, she doesn't know who she is. Husband B is strong, confident and self-assured. He assumes she is okay.

And what do you think Wife A is feeling now that she is a dot?

Yep, you know it. Resentment. Anger. Bitterness.

In some cases, depending on the amount of guilt or judgment handed her, she may feel a deep sense of shame for wanting too much or expecting too much.

And what do you think Husband B is feeling?

No, not love or appreciation or honor!

He is feeling disrespect – disrespect for the person who is like a stone underneath his shoe. Why should he respect someone so small, so insignificant and so powerless?

Geri Holmes

My dear, dear women, listen up.

Only you know what you need. Never assume he knows. And never assume that if you play Rule #3 in this game, that someday there will be some uh-huh moment and he will see and value all the surrendering you have done. Nope. It's more likely he is not playing your game, and he is not following your rules.

Only you can give yourself value – enough value to stand your ground and expect to get what you need. We are not talking about asking him for total life change. We are not talking about asking for his personality to change. We are simply asking for respect for basic human needs.

Does that mean you are demanding, naggy, bossy and controlling? Well, it could depend on your tone of voice when you ask. But hopefully you will ask for what you need quietly but firmly.

Will he always respond immediately? It is fair for him to say, "Hey honey, three minutes and the commercial is on. Can you wait?" And three minutes is a doable solution. Of course, you can wait.

Negotiation is part of living in a small room and accommodating each other.

Negotiation is what is needed to give value to BOTH people's needs.

However, did you know that sometimes BOTH people feel like the dot. These are very unhealthy dysfunctional relationships. In these relationships people live in fear of rejection, and fear of failure. Both parties are trying to navigate the three rules and play this game of purchasing love.

We need to be real, and honest. We need to be honest about who we are and what we need and what we want.

We need to accept the fact that we may sometimes come across as selfish or demanding. But we need to become the advocate for the child/person within. Who will speak on our behalf and who will give value to the way we were made?

It's gotta be you.

We began with the story of Janett and Peter. Janett needed to be clear – to say the truth about what she needed. Perhaps they could have worked it out so they both got something. Perhaps he could have stayed for the morning and let her go back to bed, and then left after lunch to bike until dark. Perhaps he could have put off his trip for another day. Perhaps. Perhaps.

But we will never know.

Need a repair in your marriage?

> Speak the truth. Stop saying, "It's okay," when it's not. Stop accommodating but then resenting it later. (Or playing the martyr and punishing him later) By standing your ground, you will learn negotiation.
>
> YOU give yourself value.
>
> I should give you a heads up though. If you start changing the way you interact with your partner, you may get some pushback. If you have allowed the other person to be maximized and yourself minimized he may be surprised and react when you start to hold your ground. But hold steady, be calm but stay firm. Restate your "no" and smile. Use humor if you can. But don't fold. Remember, to have the respect of others we first need to respect ourselves.
>
> Above all things, light a match to the game!

Geri Holmes

OWN It.

1. Which rule is most common to you?

    Rule #1: It's an act. Don't believe what women say.
    Rule #2: Read my mind. Know what I need without me telling you.
    Rule #3 – If I love you enough you will love me in return.

    Can you remember times you have played it? What was the outcome?

2. Do you feel resentment? Did you know that resentment is usually the feeling we have when we are not being honest with ourselves or others?

    When do you most often feel resentful? Towards whom?
    What is that resentment teaching you about your level of honesty?

7

Laying Down Shields

It is not possible to be in relationship for any length of time without being wounded. Most people don't mean to hurt one another but nevertheless they do.

All of us have been wounded by someone. Probably several people. And that was long before we ever met our partner.

When we are wounded we usually try to protect ourselves from it happening again.

For example, if a child reaches out to touch a candle and burns themselves, they immediately draw back. Although they are too young to understand it, their memory stores the image and warns them the next time not to touch it. This makes sense to us: what causes us pain may kill us!

Unfortunately we do this with the hurts that happen in our relationships. We keep mental notes about what was said or done and assume that by remembering the offence we will save ourselves from being hurt in the future. We "tie ourselves" to this event by holding onto the memory of the offence.

Geri Holmes

And then we raise our shields.

Shields are what we do next, after we have been wounded. Usually what our shield looks like is related to our personality, so different people have different shields. But we get used to raising our shields as children and then we keep doing the same thing in our adult relationships. It's important that we realize what shield we raise. I'll explain why in a moment.

The SHIELD of ANGER

Everyone feels some anger when hurt, but the shield of anger carries the anger and allows it to build up. They also tend to push forward into venting, raging, accusing, shaming or belittling the person who hurt them. The incident may be major or minor, but the reaction is the same. They may lie in bed at night rehearsing speeches or recalling conversations to reconstruct their responses (although they may or may not ever share their anger with the offender.) They may accumulate past mistakes and failures, linking them together to gather confidence and solidify their "right" to be angry. They may be loud or silent – lawyering or inwardly ranting.

The shield of anger says, I'll protect myself by keeping the anger alive: I'll remind you (and me) regularly of my disappointment with you so you never dare hurt me again. I'll hurt you hard to punish you so you remember what pain feels like. I'll stay angry to remind myself to not let down my guard again.

The SHIELD of SILENCE

Some people when wounded shut down. They go silent and withdraw. They become quietly passive. They feel depressed, sad or listless. Their spouse picks up on the mood change and may try to draw them out.

Tools

But the sadness holds them and their offender captive. Their silence may be a way of validating or solidifying their hurt. They may believe that by holding onto it for a long time they will reinforce how serious it really was. Or they may become silent because they believe, at some deep level that if they had been a different or better person, the offense wouldn't have happened. They feel despaired.

Either way, the worse the hurt the longer the silence. Like any shield, their silence creates tensions and distance.

The shield of silence says, I'll protect myself by feeling sad and staying sad. My sadness will put value on the depth of my hurt and by experiencing its depth I'll remind you (and me) of the pain you caused me.

The SHIELD of PERFORMANCE

Still others raise the shield of performance. When hurt, they may assume they had some part in the misunderstanding or betrayal. Or they may feel entirely responsible to reconcile quickly. So they rehearse all their past performances, what they said and did and what might have led to the current conflict and find something to apologize about. Then they may become obsessively intent on "winning them back" by being overly good and tolerant. They serve, sacrifice, and extend themselves to great lengths to prove that everything is okay. They want to restore equilibrium at any cost.

But their people-pleasing and sacrificial actions give them a sense of power over their own hurt. And it doesn't actually heal the wound; it just drives it deeper into denial. By not acknowledging the wound, the offender has no accountability in the relationship. It makes wounding even easier.

Geri Holmes

On the other hand, the offender may feel manipulated because they are being "killed with kindness." It may make them reluctant to share things in the future. It may look like forgiveness but it feels to the offender like guilty punishment.

The shield of performance says, I'll protect myself by trying harder, by purchasing your approval so you will see what a good person I am. Then this will never happen again and you will never want to hurt me again.

The SHIELD of CONTROL

This shield of self-protection involves staying vigilant and watchful. It stays alert to any sign of the past hurt occurring. The woman who raises this shield may believe she is responsible for letting her guard down. She may believe her intuition failed her. She may believe her partner made some poor choices that were avoidable if she had been on top of things. So by being watchful and "policing" their partner and his actions they protect themselves from future strikes. They may monitor the Offender's activities, over-plan, organize or orchestrate every event. They may set a plan in place to prevent any future circumstances from developing. (For example, if her partner and her have had fights during a meal she may suggest they not eat at the table anymore.) The Offender is constantly offering suggestions or critiquing others to guarantee they have all the information and are making all the right choices. If the hurt involved betrayal, the slightest hint of "dishonesty" (which may be something he simply forgot to tell you) is blown out of proportion and linked to the past hurt and pain. The offender may feel on trial and be obligated to explain their actions in depth or share thoughts and feelings without the right to say no. They may be reluctant to share how controlled them feel because the offender believes they can't be trusted again.

Tools

The shield of control says, I'll protect myself, by watching you and making sure it never happens again. I'll police you, manage your world and critique your comments because you can't be trusted again. I'll stay vigilant.

The SHIELD of BUSYNESS

One other shield is the shield of busyness. In this case the hurt person stays busy as a way to avoid thinking about the hurt and processing it. They run from the problem often to activities that are positive, sacrificial and serving. In this way they are unavailable and safe from being hurt again. They may work longer hours, go to the gym, busy themselves with kid's activities, or volunteer somewhere. Their ceaseless activity protects them from finding time alone where they may be hurt again. Because of the nobility of all this activity, the offender may feel they have no right to ask for time to reconnect or to enjoy each other's company.

The shield of busyness says, I'll protect myself by not making myself vulnerable again. And I'll make sure there is a good reason for me to be busy and unavailable.

Why do shields create problems?

First of all, it is exhausting and tiring to keep these shields in place. It takes a lot of emotional effort to stay angry or stay distant. It's physically exhausting to keep trying harder, staying busy or to keep things in control.

Second, it hurtful to the offender; they feel alone and disconnected by the distance the shield creates.

Third, it prevents the wound from being healed.

It isn't the offence that breaks us apart — it is the shield we raise to protect ourselves.

Let me repeat.

It isn't the offence that breaks us apart — it is the shield we raise to protect ourselves

Let me introduce you to Joelle and James.

James was a very handsome man who was deeply in love with Joelle, the director of corporate sales in a large real estate firm. They had been together for over five years and were considering children. One day, however, James heard Joelle's phone ping on the couch beside him signaling Joelle had a text message. He glanced over and read in the display a very provocative text message — with strong sexual content. Shocked and surprised he reached for the phone and began scrolling. (He was aware of all his partner's passwords). He saw a number of text messages from the same man — each increasingly flirtatious and intimate. Although Joelle's responses were guarded, she continued to converse with the person and affirm him.

James was angry and deeply betrayed.

When Joelle came into the room he confronted her. At first she was defensive because he looked at her phone, but then as James raged beside her, she realized the impact the messages were having on him and she cried. She was embarrassed and afraid. She deeply loved her husband.

Finally she confessed that this man was a customer who had done business with her (she was a real estate agent) on a number of transactions through the years, and was now negotiating with her on a very large property. She said she didn't have any feelings for the guy but was just trying not to offend him so that she wouldn't lose the deal. It was "harmless."

Tools

James didn't know whether or not to believe her. He was angry that she had not stopped the other guy in his tracks the first time he was flirtatious.

Joelle promised (after days of fighting) to not talk to him anymore via texts but would insist he come into the office to negotiate. James was not consoled. He wanted a 'no contact' boundary set. Let someone else handle the sale!

Over the next month he checked her phone whenever she wasn't aware. He looked for other signs of relationships. Although there were no other sexually-based texts, he noticed how friendly she was with other men and it worried him. He would confront her regularly checking what she was saying to them and why she was talking to them. Over and over she would repeat herself: "They are just customers," she would say. "I have to be friendly or I won't make any sales. And yes, sometimes the men flirt with me but it means nothing to me. I have never cheated on you and I never will!"

Two years later James had not moved on. Texting remained a constant source of tension for him. He resented her job that has introduced her to relationships with other men. Joelle worries about James and their marriage. She has become very pre-occupied with the home and keeping it tidy. She spends more time making good meals. She is cautious not to talk about work and tries hard to keep everything "light" and surface.

I'm sure you can sympathize with James. However, after two years of proven loyalty and a concerted effort on her part to be more "business like" and distant with the men she meets, he is not satisfied. She feels frustrated. She has apologized numerous times, has tried to be particularly caring and supportive in their home. She compliments him and brags on him when they were out in public. She has a large picture of him on her desk for all to see. But it is not enough. James is still angry.

The relationship was close to breaking when they sought counseling. But the culprit was not Joelle. Joelle has admittedly made some mistakes. But she has done her best to make amends.

83

Geri Holmes

It's James. James has raised his shield of control and is taking responsibility for it never happening again. He is self-protecting.

What is really needed here?

Although James has convinced himself that Joelle is to blame, his anger towards her is rooted in fear. He is afraid that she is not good enough for him. He believes in the core of his being that if he had been enough for her she would not have "welcomed" the attention of other men.

His control is his shield but his fear of inadequacy is keeping it in place. This is true for most of our shields of self-protection. Fear, hurt, feeling unsafe and unmet expectations move us to take action. But they are not helpful. When we are hurt we must acknowledge the hurt, discuss it and repair it. At some point we must forgive. The past cannot be undone. Constantly looking over our shoulders hinders our ability to move forward.

What should Joelle and James do?

If Joelle and James are to heal, first James needs to acknowledge his shield of control. He needs to acknowledge his anxiety. Then James needs to release forgiveness to Joelle for participating in provocative texts (a form of betrayal). He also needs to forgive himself for his imagined failures and let go of his self-blame. Finally, he needs to learn how to manage his anxiety without moving to control.

For Joelle to heal, she needs to lay down her "trying harder" or performance shield. She has a hard time doing this because she still carries guilt. She feels so badly she hurt her husband, and every time he drills her about her activities she sighs inside. She hates it but she deserves it. She feels so ashamed. Joelle needs to forgive herself as well.

It's time to move on. The shields are destroying the marriage. Forgiveness is needed.

Let go of shields: offer and accept forgiveness

Why is forgiveness, whether giving it or receiving it, so hard for us as human beings?

Why is so hard to lay down our self-protecting strategies?

Because we are all full of fear and full of pride.

While we admit to being human beings, we have trouble admitting to being human.

Look below at this object. Recognize it?

Right. It's a dart board.

What's the circle in the middle called?

Right again. The bull's eye.

The bull's eye is the "perfect." Hitting the middle gets you a perfect score.

Imagine a game of darts without a bull's eye. Where would you aim? How could you play?

People and life are like this dartboard.

Geri Holmes

In our hearts we seem to know what perfect looks like. We seem to know intuitively what it means to be a perfect person – a perfect father, a perfect mother, a perfect friend, a perfect spouse.

Think about it. Perfect people always show you kindness and patience. They believe in you, trust you, encourage you, listen attentively to all your needs. They speak the truth to help you grow but never harshly or with meanness. They protect you, have your back and carefully tend you when you are sick. And so on.

And yet who does that all the time?

Even the best people fail occasionally. They act too quickly or not quickly enough. They overindulge us at times, or over correct. They work too hard and are not available to us or set the standard so high we feel inadequate.

You see, all of us, in the game of life, fall short of the mark. All of us are imperfect.

Can I repeat that a different way - there are NO PERFECT PEOPLE!

And yet we need the bull's eye in order to know where to aim. We carry perfect in our heart to keep us trying, moving forward and growing.

But unfortunately we measure ourselves against it. And we compare ourselves to others.

We see other people's darts land way off the board – those dysfunctional people with addictions or abusers etc. We compare ourselves to them and we think, "I'm not that bad. No, I'm better than THAT!"

And perhaps we are. Perhaps our dart lands closer to the center, closer to the perfect.

Tools

And yet are we better?

The truth is that no matter where our dart lands we will have disappointed someone. We will have offended someone, hurt someone or failed someone.

Not because we meant to but just because we do! We have missed the mark. We are human.

Through life, from one year to the next, through learning from our mistakes, by adjusting our aim we may do better. We are always growing up.

But never quite "there!"

What do we need? More practice? Yes, of course.

But what we need even more is forgiveness. Kindness. Grace.

We need the ones we interact with to love us, forgive us and allow us room to grow – to accept our humanity – and sometimes the stupid things we do.

And most importantly, we need to acknowledge our own failure and allow ourselves to be okay with our own immaturity and humanity.

There's a gap between the bulls eye and where the dart lands. There's a gap between where we are and where we wish to be. And its okay!

But there's more.

People who struggle with forgiveness – either giving it or receiving it – lack one thing.

They lack humility.

Geri Holmes

Those that find it hardest to forgive are hardest on themselves. Like an abusive coach, they beat themselves up with regularity. They set the standard high. They won't settle for anything but determined, practiced effort.

Unfortunately this incessant beating ourselves up doesn't work.

If we are going to have lasting relationships we must lower the bar. Lower the standard. We must acknowledge at the deepest level of our life we have all missed the mark.

And so have they!

That makes room in our hearts to forgive others. To ease off. To expect less and be pleasantly surprised when we get more.

There is a mantra in sports I actually despise. It is, 'Always do your best.'

Really? Who always does their best? And what if my best today is not my best tomorrow? What if I'm tired, or disinterested, or exhausted? Why must I always do my best?

Expecting less does not mean we will stop trying. We will forever carry perfect in our hearts.

But expecting less means reviewing our performance, responding to our regrets with mental notes. And then throwing out the dart again! Practice. Practice.

However, in the meantime, every day of our lives, we need to forgive.

How?

Tools

Forgiveness is not a feeling and it's not earned over time. Once we have wounded another we can never go back to the way it was before. When we have hurt someone we can never undo the damage by "making it up" to them. We must learn from our mistakes, of course. We must look deeply at ourselves to understood what motivated that behavior or what circumstances contributed to making the choices we did. And we can confess that.

But at some point we need to let it go and move on. That's true of when I hurt others, and its true of when others hurt me.

How do we forgive others?

We make a decision.

Forgiveness is a choice to cancel debts. Just as I cease making payments if my bank debt was forgiven, so I cease requiring payments when I forgive another. When the thought or reminder of the past offense arrives, ringing the doorbell in my brain, I send the butler to not allow it admittance. I tell myself with firm resolve, "I am not going there. I have forgiven that offence and I will not remind myself of it again." I refuse to entertain it, invite it inside my conscious thought and serve it tea. I shake my head, distract myself or shut my mouth and refuse to respond.

I make a decision and I hold myself to it.

If we do not learn to forgive we will become bitter. And there is nothing that will poison a person and steal their love more than bitterness. It is a poison we swallow hoping others die.

I began this chapter addressing the shields we raise when we are hurt. I ended the chapter with a look at forgiveness. These may seem like two different topics. However, they are deeply connected.

89

Geri Holmes

I personally believe it is impossible to lay down our shields of self-protection after being hurt unless we see a solution for our pain. As I mentioned earlier, it is our instinct to survive that causes us to self-protect. We are afraid of our own vulnerability. Who will save us if we do not save ourselves?

However, even though it is "natural" to hold offences, it is ineffective in relationships. Shields divide. Shields create distance. Shields change the nature of the "dance" we have with each other.

We must allow ourselves to risk again. We must become vulnerable once more.

As women it's vital we share honestly and transparently what actions or behaviors hurt us, and the impact of the hurt on us. Of course we are hoping for some understanding and a heartfelt apology.

Unfortunately we don't always get it. Why? Human beings get caught up in their own needs, their own goals, and their own desires. As a result while barreling ahead to get those needs, goals or desires met they hurt the people they love the most.

Secondly, so much of our behavior is rooted in immaturity, ignorance or just old habits. No matter how old we are, we are all "growing up." We need room to grow and so does our partner.

I believe Joelle learned her lesson. Her fear of losing money got the better of her and she allowed personal compromise. I doubt very much Joelle will entertain or encourage sexual conversations again. But will James believe in her ability to grow, learn and change? Will James forgive and trust again? That is James' choice – not Joelle's.

If you don't want to do damage to your marriage swallow your pride, embrace your own humanity with its vulnerabilities and release yourself of pride and perfection – and forgive!

Need a repair in your marriage?

> Lay down your shields and forgive. It's the greatest gift we give. It is the most undeserving gift we receive.

OWN it.

1. What shield is most familiar to you? Can you find a memory of when you used it? How effective was it at helping you resolve an issue? Is it still in place?

   Look behind the shield – what did you feel first, BEFORE you raised it. Can you find those emotions and share them. Journal them in your notebook.

   What would it be like for you to process those feelings and acknowledge them? What would it be like for you to accept hurt and woundedness as part of life?

2. Set some time aside, at least two hours when you know you will not be interrupted. Grab your notebook and begin to think: think back to the very beginning when you met your spouse.

   What are the hurts, and offences you still remember?

   Make some notes in your journal.

   After you have made your note, ask yourself – am I ready to forgive this? It may be small but why are you holding onto the memory? Can you write beside it – Today, I choose to forgive _____ for _____.

   Go to the next memory, small or large. Do the same.

Geri Holmes

Progress through the months and years and write what you remember that is negative and hurtful. Each time, choose to forgive.

When done, review the list, and one final time make a strong and clear statement: Today on _____ (date) I choose to forgive you _____(name) for these hurts and offenses. Today I choose to put a Butler at the door of my mind so that when a thought or reminder comes I choose to not entertain it. I cancel all debts and expected payments for this offense. I will not bring these debts up again. I will not connect them to any present or future offense. I cut _____(name) free.

8

Owning One's Happiness

There can be many reasons why a woman chooses to get together with a man and have a relationship. The one I hear the most is, "He makes me happy."

On a similar note, when a couple's relationship is distressed they may consider breaking up. The number one reason I hear is, "I'm not happy anymore."

Occasionally I will give a stack of "value cards" to a client. Each card has a different value on it such as security, traditions, freedom, or family. I ask the client to sort the cards and order them from most important to the least important. I have noted that quite often the "happiness" card is in the top three values.

These responses concern me. Why?

Happiness is a feeling not a foundation.

Feelings are fickle, changeable and unreliable. That is why they do not work as a foundation on which to decide things.

Have you ever had someone sneak up behind you and startle you with a giant "boo." In those first few seconds your fingers tingle, your heart

Geri Holmes

races and you nearly pass out from the sudden drop in blood flow to the brain.

Stop the camera. Freeze the scene.

Every single indication in your body says there is danger. Your adrenal gland is pumping because it is convinced there is a threat. Your heart rate has increased. You feel instantly alert and may even immediately sweat. Run. Fight. You are not safe.

But is there a real threat?

No threat. Just your nasty little cousin scaring you again! When you realize who it is, new messages enter the brain. It's okay. All is well. Relax. As those new messages hit the brain the body relaxes. The heart returns to normal.

With this simple illustration we understand that feelings can't always be trusted. And feelings change quickly with new ideas.

Nevertheless, all feelings are valid, even if they can't be trusted. Feelings are there to help us, to alert us, to warn us, and to encourage us to take action. If we were never angry, would we ever rise to defend the victim? If we were never worried, would we ever make mid-course corrections to forestall a disaster?

But emotions are not there to speak for us, to pre-determine our choices or assume they hold sway over what happens next. It is possible to be unhappy for a season, sometimes even a long time, and to use that feeling to evaluate what is going on inside of yourself or in your life. Unhappiness can help you to address problems or seek solutions. Many times our unhappiness is there to help us to change.

Happiness is subjective and uniquely experienced by each individual.

Tools

Many things can affect a woman's emotions in the here and now. Her health. Her menstrual cycle or menopause. How her children behave and how she interacts with them. Extended family can be a problem. Workplace stress. Too many things to do and not enough time to do them. The loss of a loved one. A broken friendship. Any or all of these things can increase a woman's feelings of unhappiness or discontent.

It is natural to turn to your spouse for understanding.

A spouse may be a good listener. A spouse may be a kind and comforting responder. But he is not responsible for your emotion. He is not responsible to keep you happy or make you happy.

Especially when what makes you unhappy is an echo to the past.

Many times the reason we are overwhelmed by certain feelings is because it reminds us of another time when we felt the same thing – perhaps when helpless, powerless or overwhelmed. Typically we dislike that emotion.

Susie was left alone a lot. She was raised by a working mother and an absent workaholic father. She was frequently anxious and afraid because mom would emphatically tell her to keep the doors locked when she was gone. Susie hated being alone. She hated being ignored. When she was ignored or alone she felt anxious.

Years later Susie is in a committed relationship. When she first got married her spouse worked long hours but was home every night. Recently however, her spouse received a promotion that meant he has to attend to clients and meetings in far away places. She is left alone. Susie is very unhappy during these times; worried, anxious and even angry. Her and her spouse have had a number of major blowouts because of his job. He won't quit. She feels abandoned.

Geri Holmes

But the problem isn't the marriage or working long hours – it's Susie's sensitivity to being alone. Nearby she has supportive family and friends. She has a busy career of her own. But when her husband leaves for work she is "triggered."

What Susie needs to do is unpack her fear of being alone and develop a new sense of empowerment and capability in handling that emotion. She needs to adjust her beliefs: she is not that little girl anymore, helpless and overwhelmed by a set of circumstances that she had no control over. She is an adult. She can reach out. She can go out. She can call a friend. But to manage herself she needs to understand the root of her unhappiness.

I had a friend who had experienced severe physical abuse as a child. If I came up behind him, touched his shoulder or back without warning, he would whip around and raise his fist to hit me. He had been known for throwing a punch at a friend. The average person would not react in that way. Why did he? His history with fear had increased his startle response.

So when I, not knowing his condition approached him and touched him, he responded in anger. Even though he was angry I was not responsible for his reaction. I apologized once I knew his story but not because I was responsible. My apology just showed empathy.

In the same way we all have "baggage." We all have some sort of history with a feeling that we dislike.

Some people hate being ignored, being alone, being rejected, or being criticized. Other people hate it when they think they have hurt someone's feelings or disappointed someone.

Because of our past experience with this emotion we are very reactive and defensive when triggered by our spouse or an event in the

Tools

relationship. It's easy to blame the partner because of our sensitivity to these feelings.

For example spouses have been known to say, "You know if bothers me when I'm left alone, so why didn't you call me?" Or, "You know I get uncomfortable when you speak to another woman because my first partner cheated on me."

It's unfortunate that many times we pay the debt forward and expect our spouses to compensate for past disappointments and pain.

But managing our own stuff is hard enough – trying to manage someone else's is impossible.

That's why happiness has to be my responsibility.

And that brings me to what my experience has found: the three most common reasons women blame their men or their marriages for their unhappiness.

1. You don't support me.

Many women have the mistaken belief that a man should be their comforter, their soother, their comic relief, their housekeeper, their child minder and "anything else I need you to be for me right now."

Wanting to share our distresses with others is natural. Every spouse expects a certain measure of comforting from their partner when they are distressed. But part of maturing in life is accepting the responsibility for comforting ourselves, developing a network of resources, exploring our spiritual options and recognizing that no matter how much we wish it, it is unlikely that any human being will fully understand what is happening within us.

Geri Holmes

Unfortunately, I have observed many women become angry or resentful when their husband failed to say the right words, hug her, hold her, or take the things that stress her off her plate. And in that moment he became the problem.

This is called "projection."

A classic example of projection is what Margaret did when she lost her husband to cancer.

Margaret had been to the emergency with him a number of times to identify the severe pain in his body. But the cause of the pain was a mystery. Medical professionals suggested it could be different things. They tried various medicines and treatments. There was no improvement. Finally on the last visit, after five months of hospital and doctor's visits, it was determined he had cancer.

However it was too late to operate. He was gone within two weeks.

Margaret was so angry. She wrote letters to the hospital, obtained all the records including the names of every doctor, lab technician and other treatment professional. She had formulated letters to be sent, determined to have licenses revoked and jobs suspended for incompetence. She came to see me with a large portfolio full of all the documentation she had gathered. Yes, Margaret was very angry.

Through the course of the counseling we talked about her husband, how she missed him, how her children missed him, how her life had changed and she grieved deeply. Slowly she stopped mentioning the incompetence of the hospital and the campaign she had begun in favor of discussions around how she was changing her lifestyle to accommodate being alone. Over time she let it all go because she recognized in her grief that she was projecting her anger onto the hospital.

And this is a common grief reaction.

Tools

And like her, we "project" too – for all kinds of different reasons. We project onto our husbands our powerlessness, frustration, tiredness and angst. We make him responsible for all that ails us. Fix me. Heal me. Believe in me.

And we project our unhappiness onto the marriage.

Why? Because frankly its hard to take responsibility for the choices we make, and sometimes we don't know how to find our way out of poor decisions or overwhelming feelings.

Many women enter marriage with the, "I can have it all" approach, including "I can be everything." Many women's expectations of themselves, their home, their financial status, their family connection and yes, of their husband are unrealistic. And because of it they are greatly overburdened and overwhelmed.

My heart goes out to these women because sometimes life just snowballs. And sometimes we were just young and foolish. It's important to stop when we are unhappy and ask ourselves what we have control over. What decisions did we make and what decisions can we make now?

Lacy and Kevin live on an acreage. They have three children, one in hockey, one in dance, and a young one still in daycare. They have a beautiful home but the yard is a work in progress. The lawn is large enough to take six hours of mowing every ten days – something Kevin usually does. But because of his additional overtime, Lacy has picked it up.

They have two relatively new vehicles, both requiring payments. Their credit cards aren't crazy but still high enough that they have to be careful to keep on top of the payments each month or they will be up to their limit. The house has a fairly high mortgage.

They bought the house after Lacy decided to go from part-time to full-time.

Geri Holmes

Lacy is experiencing anxiety and at times she is panicking. She is exhausted most of the time, especially on the weekends when Kevin's child from a previous marriage comes to visit. She tries to make the time more special and plan things to do with his child. Some of these outings include more time with his family so his child can keep in touch with her grandparents. Some of these outings include the hockey trips, soccer trips and dance recitals. Some of these trips cost a lot of money.

Lacy began getting angry about a year ago. She began resenting Kevin's child. The home was overwhelming to keep clean and Kevin would frequently try to coach her in how to be more organized to keep the place cleaner. Why didn't he just clean it then, she thought. She felt criticized and pressured. That was before she took up the summer lawn project.

Lately, she has refused Kevin's advances and has gone to bed without him. She is tired. The distance is growing between them and Kevin seems to spend less time helping out and more time at work.

She struggles with the urge to run: "We need to get away," she says. "We need down time with the kids. Maybe even a holiday without them."

She lays in bed thinking. About their life. About his lack of support. About his selfishness in being gone all the time. About the way he seems to prioritize his child and not her. She starts wondering if she wants this marriage any more. Lacy is unhappy.

So what do you think needs to be done? Is she unhappy with Kevin? Should she leave the relationship?

Could her unhappiness and stress be telling her something? Could it be her unhappiness is helping her to identify a life stretched to the limits?

The truth is Lacy and Kevin had made many decisions that brought her to this point. She wanted the bigger house so they got the bigger mortgage. She dreamed of an acreage where her kids could experience

100

Tools

what she did growing up on a farm. When her car needed to be replaced she wanted all the latest gadgets. But that meant more work and less money. She offered and cooperated with outings and excursions.

Pleasing others, over-extending herself and her finances, idealistic dreams, wanting everything now, not being comfortable with having less – all of these affected her happiness. And she needs to own it before she can begin to change it.

Sometimes just owning it changes it.

I remember a day when my children were young. I had decided to homeschool them for a number of reasons. I was excitedly committed to this project. I loved teaching and I loved having more involvement in my children's lives. My husband, who was normally passive, smiled and agreed that it was a great idea. Of course, that meant I would not hold a full-time job.

Unfortunately my husband made barely enough money to put a roof over our heads. It was difficult financially. This limited the number of things I could do with the children because of financial restrictions. But to me the kids were more important than money.

One day I was in a funk – unhappy, frustrated, angry and discouraged. I compared my husband to other home-schooling dads I knew and the money they could generate. I complained inwardly about his self-employment: his lack of planning, lack of good spending or saving habits, and the fact he was gone a lot to find work or do the work. He didn't do anything with the kids to "support" me in the homeschooling.

But then it dawned on me.

I chose this. It was my idea. I had done the research. I had made the decision. When I shared it with my husband he said he would support

101

Geri Holmes

me. But there was no clear understanding of what "support" looked like.

The truth was it was primarily my decision and my choice.

As I pondered this reality, I weighed my options: I could put them in school. I could get a job. I could change our financial bottom line.

I could actually end this stress. It was my choice!

By taking responsibility for my happiness I chose again – to keep doing the same thing I was doing and settle it in my heart. This was my life. This was my husband. This was my marriage. I loved my husband. I loved my kids. I needed to decide to love my life.

Sometimes that's enough.

Or sometimes, like Lacy, you may need to make some hard decisions – decisions to go backwards – to a smaller house, to a smaller mortgage, to a cheaper vehicle, to less work and a quieter life. Many times hard decisions involve not keeping up with the status quo, not giving our children everything other's do, accepting that our means do not match others.

2. The grass is greener

A second reason why women blame their men or marriage for their unhappiness is as the sub-title states: the grass is greener.

In my experience, couples can work through almost anything in a marriage – addictions, blending families, mettlesome in-laws, sexual dysfunctions, financial disasters and even sometimes affairs - if there is a commitment to each other.

Tools

But not everyone who comes for counseling is in that committed place. Typically, if one partner is unmotivated, and is emphatically "done," we cannot reconcile the relationship.

When one of the individuals in the relationship is unwilling to work on it, I have learned to ask this question: "Who is in your life right now that has a greater appeal than your partner?"

I am not asking the question assuming they are in an affair. All I am asking is if someone else is looking good. If either person has started looking around, or has met someone who has caught their eye or given them the attention or affection they feel they are lacking, quite frequently it becomes the tipping point. The marriage feels impossible, the problems are insurmountable and the effort just isn't there. A marriage can be a 5/10, or a 7/10 but when another man catches a woman's eye, the needle drops dramatically.

A woman might meet a man at work who is attentive, listening and understanding. She may have a good friend who has a husband that seems so much better than hers – more helpful, available and involved. She may have a family member whom she connects with and feels so relaxed and "herself" with. She may have reconnected with an old boyfriend from high school that is on her social media and who reminds her she is still hot.

Once you start comparing the grass, the other grass looks better.

And the problems that were always there suddenly became unbearable.

That habit that has annoyed you for ten years is now a problem because he doesn't care.

That "beer belly" that you actually thought once was kind of cute is now disgusting and obnoxious.

Geri Holmes

And that other guy, the one without the belly, and without that habit, or who has no family problems - he would be so much easier to live with.

Cheating begins in the heart and the head, not in the bed.

The good news is when individuals acknowledge they have been looking and dreaming, imagining or fantasizing they are ready to begin. To find their way back to their marriage they need to break all connections and shut off their mind to any other option. They need to guard their heart and quit looking over the fence.

An anonymous study was done of people who were divorced for at least five years and in a second relationship. The question was asked, "Are you happier now?" Every person, other than those who had been in a domestic violence situation said No. Their explanation was, they didn't get something better. They just got something different. Old stressors were gone, but new ones had been added.

Trust me on this. The grass is seldom greener: it's just a different yard.

3. I need it NOW

The final thing that robs us of our happiness in the marriage is impatience.

I remember when I was young a speaker at a woman's conference drew a circle on the board and labeled it, "A Woman's Life." She drew lines to cut it into bits like pieces of a pie. The total pie represented about 80+ years (the average life-expectancy of a woman in Canada)

The first piece represented approximately 22 years – the years of childhood, school and getting an education. This was approximately one-fourth of her life.

Tools

The next piece represented the years after she married – the years of having children and raising them. This piece of the pie represented another twenty years of her life (A very busy piece of pie!)

But then the speaker made a very powerful statement that caught my attention:

Only one half of a woman's life was spent.

The rest of her life, that second half, was all hers. The years in the second half were hers in which to develop her career, pursue her dreams and spend more time with her friends doing the things she loved.

As a young mom this impacted me. It gave me the bigger picture.

Many times as a young mom I felt trapped. I felt stunted in my personal growth. I felt discouraged by my small house, and low finances. I felt my career wasn't going anywhere.

I was discontented with all of it. Why?

Because I wanted it all NOW.

I had lost perspective of the whole of my life.

I truly believe that one of the things that has created so much unrest and unhappiness in women is impatience. We want material things such as a big house, nice car, vacations, clothes, personal perks and recreation. So we work ourselves to the bone to have it now.

We want the joys of children, quality time, involvements in sports or activities that create family time yet foster and develop our children's talents. So we use every second of our time to have it now.

Geri Holmes

We want the recognition of careers, accomplishments and promotions so we invest the best hours of our day giving ourselves away. We give what's left to the kids and the husband.

Until there's not anything left of our real selves to give.

Then we seek a break. And so we crave the freedom for personal time, coffee with the girls, retreats, spas and leisurely things. Unfortunately those things cost money and it takes time. So we squeeze and we squeeze every second of our time and our cash until our emotional selves register either guilt and resentment or anxiety and depression. Unfortunately for some, substances or fantasies become a needed escape.

Raising kids is hard work and very time consuming. Sometimes the marriage suffers - not because people don't love each other but because all this busyness is very demanding. Then we hear things like, "If you don't stay in touch with each other, one day you will wake up and you won't even know each other." And so another expectation is added.

Impatience and the need to have it all now is a great drain on happiness. And a great drain on the marriage.

Remember when I talked about the dartboard? What if we allowed ourselves to be a B-minus person who decides *not* to be everything to everybody now? What if we accepted ourselves as a B-minus mom – because that is the best we could do right now! What if we decided to turn down some career opportunities and be a B-minus employee? What if we accepted that our life was still good even when it wasn't all we wished it to be? What if we were contented with (shudder shudder) average?

Need a repair in your marriage?

> Take charge of your own happiness. Review your past decisions and your present circumstances and take ownership for the choices you now have.
>
> Second, stop looking over the fence. Focus on the positives in your own back yard. You've worked a long time on making it grow, so don't give up now. Most everything can be improved with hard work and determination.
>
> Finally, acknowledge your impatience and make more realistic goals. Life can still be good even when it's not great.

OWN it.

Stop for a moment and ponder, What in your life are you not happy about?

1. Have another look at your past experiences: family of origin, bullies, dates, past relationships. What feelings do you hate? What circumstances "trigger" you? Pick one feeling/issue that is hard for you and get some help. Don't assume your spouse should be the one to fix it for you.

2. Have you been guilty of looking across the fence? What is it that is attracting you there? Be real and honest. Now consider, what is good about your grass: this man you are living with? Focus on the positives. Develop a daily routine of listing what is good.

3. Are you impatient? Make a list of all the things you want in life now. Once done (it will be a long one!) prioritize. What is absolutely essential and what is a 'want' but not a need. Focus on the top 5 or 6 and make a decision to let go and wait for the rest – for now.

9

Redefining Commitment

So you decided to get married, or perhaps not legally married but living common-law.

It may be your first relationship, your second, or some other number after, but this relationship is important to you. And I am assuming if you picked up this book, you want your relationship to last.

That's why we need to start at the beginning.

The beginning might determine the outcome.

Could we be sabotaging the relationship before we even start?

So then, what's the beginning?

Simply put, it's the commitment. People identify themselves to me as a "committed couple." This is their beginning.

But what does that mean?

How do we define it?

Tools

For some people commitment is simply exclusivity. It's me saying, "If I catch you with anyone else it's over."

But actually that's not a commitment; that's a contract.

A contract is not the same as a commitment.

- A contract has conditions - it's a list of expectations. And those conditions can be measured and evaluated and decided on.

If the demands, conditions or expectations are not eventually met, the contract is broken, and the relationship dissolves.

For example, if you fail to make payments to the bank for your car loan, the contract is over. Your relationship with the car terminates.

The bank has made no "commitment" to you and your car needs. They are unsympathetic to your plight and show no mercy. Why? Because the conditions of payment were agreed upon at the beginning! When you don't meet them they seize the car.

While some people say marriage is just a piece of paper, real marriage, the kind that lasts is quite different.

It is a commitment. Not a contract.

In fact, it has nothing to do with paper or what's written down.

- Marriage is the making of a new unit or a living thing.

Let me explain.

When we were children we were under the care of a mother and father. We were enmeshed or interconnected within their lives. We had very little say, or "autonomy." Most likely we ate what they cooked, went to bed when they said and went to school whether we wanted to or not.

109

But there was a plus to this: we were in a family. And in that family our basic needs were met – needs for food, clothing and shelter, needs for love and needs for belonging.

Our family unit wasn't built on a contract because we were dependent. It was built on a parental commitment to meet our needs.

Notice the three circles below. The larger two circles represent the parents, and the smaller circle represents the child.

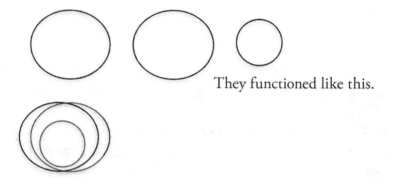

They functioned like this.

Our circle or our "self" is underneath their circles and enmeshed into the family unit.

Then we "launched." We left the circle of care, and developed our own independence. We achieved "autonomy." Perhaps we went to university, or found a job. Perhaps we got our own apartment. But what distinguished us as an adult was that we made choices of our own and learned we could be our "own person." We were disengaged from our parents. We were independent.

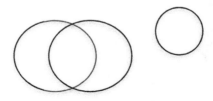

Then we "marry." We find another and we join together.

But this new unit doesn't look like our first home, when we were dependent and living with our parents. (Enmeshed) Neither does it look like when we were independent and living on our own. (Disengaged) On the contrary, this relationship or unit looks entirely different.

Notice the shaded area. It's where the two circles overlap making it a third, new entity.

This is the marriage. It exists as part of both of us, and yet it has an identity of its own.

It exists because of the investment each person makes into the new unit.

- Marriage is not like a contract because it is an investment

Just like two living beings join together and make a child, two committed people join together to make a marriage. Like a child, it is something made up of both of them, and yet it exists on its own. And that child, from the day it is conceived requires our investment AND our commitment.

Even when a child is difficult to raise and demands a lot of us we do not abandon it. We do not stop investing. Why? The child is part of us. And we are committed to it.

Geri Holmes

Marriage is like that. As we invest, nurture and care for it, it becomes part of us.

And we don't abandon it when it feels hard, or when it's taking a lot to keep it alive.

Once a child is conceived there is no way to measure what attributes came from what person. Neither can you measure each person's contribution to a marriage.

In fact marriage can't be measured at all.

And that is why it is very different than a contract.

Very early in a relationship a woman may get angry. She's having one of "those" days. She feels used, alone and forgotten. She counts the number of times she agreed or surrendered to her partner's wants or wishes. She counts the times she sacrificed and served her Significant Other. She starts measuring her efforts against his efforts. The scale feels unbalanced.

But the minute she begins to think this way she has moved from a commitment to a contract.

Imagine a mother keeping a record of how often she fed her child, or how many meals she prepared, diapers she changed or sheets she washed. Why would she? It's what you do to nurture your baby.

And so it is with marriage.

You may be concerned that I am suggesting only one person can keep a marriage alive. On the contrary, just as it takes two people to make a child, it takes two to properly raise one. Healthy marriages require investments from both parties.

Tools

This brings me to the second difference between commitment and contract.

- Marriage is not fair. Marriage is not built on a foundation of fairness.

Now I realize that many people who get married may still not have a marriage mindset. They are contractual in their thinking. In fact they are bringing a mindset to the marriage that I call the "common-law curse."

The common-law curse is when we believe everything is 50/50 and equally shared.

For example, when a couple moves in together typically both have jobs, (or are expected to get one) so they share the costs like roommates do. This may include splitting the rent, or dividing up the home bills. It may include splitting the grocery costs or 'you pay for this and I'll pay for that.' They split their time – your friends and my friends. If either person complains about something not being fair, it is argued and resolved.

After some time, as many relationships evolve, a decision is made to buy a home perhaps or have a baby. If they get pregnant, money may decrease depending on whether the wife has maternity leave or unemployment benefits.

Her energy decreases. Her moods may change.

Babies require a lot of time and energy: the care and upkeep of the home may deteriorate - she may not be able to hold up her half of the equation. She may feel overwhelmed.

In many ways she feels like she is giving more, and in other ways, perhaps financially or sexually, she is giving less.

113

Geri Holmes

Men on the other hand, may add extra work to fill the financial gap. They make work longer or harder. They are less available, more tired, less helpful. Or they may just keep doing what they were doing but in contrast to everything she is doing, it now seems not enough.

Or maybe everyone is trying "equally" as hard but both are exhausted, tired and more "demanding."

What do we do now? Things don't seem fair.

And so we may get out the scorecard. We evaluate whether what's happening is reasonable and fair. We see some problems.

For example, he doesn't think its fair that he has to work so hard, help in the house and do her errands when she is home all the time doing "nothing."

She doesn't think it's fair that he is gone so much, that the lion's share of the childcare falls on her. He gets to go out more, see his friends more, and leave whenever he feels like it. She has to stay home while the child naps, or is cutting teeth.

Resentment sets in as each person begins to measure. Fights may escalate and end with, "Well, why don't you just leave then." The contractual view of the relationship results in insecurity, fear and the pressure to measure up as each person keeps score.

Scorekeeping is simply monitoring fairness. It is making sure they match each other in giving and serving.

When we are scorekeeping we are always disappointed, and the nature of the relationship becomes a competition.

We compete to be the same and do the same things. Time to ourselves. Time with our friends. Time to work out. Money to pamper ourselves.

Tools

Money for entertainment. These are just a few of the things that we calculate, compare and compete for.

When relationships divide it is almost always because one or the other feels their effort, their work or their share is more than the other person's.

Which is why, if you want to stay together and make it work, you must confront the common-law curse.

If you insist on a relationship built on fairness you are setting it up to fail.

How does marriage really work? (And this brings us back to what commitment really means.)

To be committed means at times we give more than we get

No you heard me right. I did say you give more. In fact it will cost you more than when you were single - maybe not in money but in effort, in time, in sacrifice and in serving. Its not a free ride, good sex, cheap housing, and friendship on demand.

And it's not like it was when we lived at home. We are no longer a dependent. So we can't expect to be taken care of.

And it's not like it was when we lived alone. We are no longer independent. So we can't just do our own thing and live for ourselves.

To be committed means we make a one-sided commitment to love

Most often, as part of a commitment to marriage people make vows. The typical old vows promised to love and to cherish in sickness and in health, in joy or in sorrow, for better, for worse, for richer for poorer.

115

Geri Holmes

Vows may have changed but they all include one thing - the promise to love. Even common-law couples commit to love.

But how can we promise or commit to a feeling? The truth is that no relationship is ever always good. And no one is ever always happy. And no one always feels love. We've talked about some of this already.

And so what do we do when we don't "feel it."

What if we have stopped being "in love?"

What if we stopped being "happy?"

That's why marriage is different. When we commit to a marriage we commit to doing what marriage requires. We commit to tending the new unit or living thing called marriage. We keep investing in the 'other.' We don't cash in.

Imagine the new unit called marriage as a plant. It is dry and shriveled up from lack of watering and care giving. We've been busy perhaps, distracted and tired and we've neglected it. As a result there are no flowers or buds, just dry, dull leaves.

But then we begin to water again, perhaps give it some fertilizer.

Suddenly one day we are surprised to find a bud. Soon, the bud opens and we discover a flower.

And that is how the feeling of love works in a marriage.

Love is first an action. It's a choice and a verb. It is not a feeling.

But feelings follow actions.

In fact love is actually a hundred choices.

Tools

To be committed means we keep doing what love requires.

Like a parental commitment we must keep giving, stay with it and not bail even when the feeling isn't there.

So when he asks me for something, we try to respond generously. Technically we are saying yes to him, but actually we are also saying yes to "it." We're doing it for the marriage. We're doing it for our future, our home, and for the stability and joy our child needs. And yes, indirectly we are doing it for ourselves.

Because we still need marriage. We need the life it brings, the covering it provides, the security and safety it provides for our children and ourselves. We want the plant and the blooms it produces. And we want it for a life-time!

To be committed means we "do" love whether we "feel" love or not

But what if the marriage feels dead, you may ask. What if I love someone else?

Remember our discussion on the grass is greener?

Sarah was working in a job that she really loved. She had a stable income that was refreshing because she had lived for many years with financial hardship. She was affirmed and valued in her job.

And then she had a conflict, a misunderstanding between her and the boss. Sarah became afraid and anxious. She didn't want to lose this job.

So even though she didn't believe she was in the wrong in the misunderstanding that happened, she determined to win her boss's approval. Sarah determined to convince him he had her all wrong he just needed to see what an amazing person she was. She hoped this would guarantee her job security.

117

Geri Holmes

So she focused on him. A lot. She learned what got his attention, what made him smile. She supported his efforts, she praised him, she worked hard for him. And one day, while sitting in a staff meeting Sarah realized something. She loved him.

One problem.

Sarah was already married.

Sarah was actually quite shocked and disappointed in herself. She was a woman with good moral character who believed in marital faithfulness. But her feelings were very real and very strong. She seriously considered ending her own marriage because of it. After all, the feelings she had for her boss were much stronger than the ones (if any) she was feeling for her husband.

She didn't realize it at the time, but much of Sarah's feelings came from the fact that she had been investing in the relationship with her boss. Sarah got back what she invested in. She gave and she saw a return – something Sarah had not done for many years in her own marriage. The marriage plant was pathetic.

Through disappointments and hurt Sarah had withdrawn her giving efforts. She did her duty but no more. She had been scorekeeping for years. Although she had no plans to leave, she had already decided she was deserving of better. Truthfully it was much easier to give to this new man than to give to the man she was married to.

The good news was Sarah and her partner sought help. And they found their way back.

Love did return to the marriage when they focused again on giving. But first Sarah had to let go of old offences (burn the scorecards!) And both had to realize they were taking the relationship for granted. They were giving very little to keep it alive.

Tools

Some people would have given up when they awoke without love in their marriage. Some people would have assumed they missed it - they failed to find their soul mate. Some people would have calculated the contractual expectations and concluded it was over.

But love follows what love does. Like Sarah, the feeling of love, of attraction, of desire, of closeness and connection came as a direct result of whom she focused on and on whom she directed her love.

It is surprising to many people that the way to love again is to give again.

We assume the way to love again is to be loved – and so we demand love to be given to us. And until we get what we think we need, we withhold the little we have. This withholding dance just saps any chance for recovery and speeds up the dying process.

However, the opposite is true. We love again by investing in faith. As we nurture the plant the bloom will appear. If there is no scorekeeping, how much we give is not measured against how much he gives. We just give out of our need. Someone once said, if you do not have enough for what you need, than let what you have be your seed.

Of course I recognize that both parties must be involved, as was the case with Sarah and her partner. And I recognize that one may have faith and refocus and the other may not. We cannot manage another person's choices.

And yet I have seen one partner's efforts kick start a new pattern of love and recovery.

So lets' review and evaluate.

- Contractual people give a little and then measure the response before proceeding.

- Contractual people keep score and recall all past failures. They compare and compete.
- Contractual people base their relationship on feelings not actions.

But true commitment – the kind that results in long-lasting and long-term relationships is a life-long investment in a new unit and a living thing. It is 'doing' even when we don't feel it.

Need a repair in your marriage?

> Review your commitment and consider your promises. Be ready to invest all you can and all you have, to love and to cherish from this day forward.
>
> Burn the scorecards. Forget fairness. Give more.
>
> It's my observation your relationship is not thriving unless you feel and believe you are giving more, much more than your partner. And that is as it should be. The plant will thrive and love will blossom.

OWN it.

1. Take a moment to write down what expectations you had of a committed relationship – of what he would do and what you would do? Then ask yourself:

How am I doing now? Have I always given what I believed I would? What would you hope your partner would think or feel about you? How do you hope he will act towards you when you fail to meet those expectations?

Tools

2. Have you found yourself adopting the lens of fairness in your relationship? Do you find yourself comparing what you have done versus what he has done? Do you have mental scorecards? If so:

   What would happen if you let them go?
   What are you afraid will happen?
   Where do you believe those fears come from?
   Have you ever recognized those fears and talked to someone about them?

3. Do you find this annoying or fearful - this unselfish view of giving to a marriage? Why? What does it reveal about your past expectations of marriage?

10

Reconnecting with God

If you are not a "religious" person, you may wonder why I am including this chapter as part of my bag of tools for repairing your marriage. Let me explain.

I believe that at some point in everyone's life we come to the end of ourselves. We may be overwhelmed, anxious or empty. Or we may be frustrated, angry or depressed. Typically we feel unsupported and alone. Our marriage partner has failed or is failing us by not being available for some reason. Our friends are either tired of our venting or leave us feeling worse because of their unsympathetic responses. Our family, good or bad, can't always be there. Our thoughts include, "I don't think I can do this anymore."

Because of this sense of alienation and emptiness we may feel helpless and hopeless. Why stay in a marriage when, "you give me nothing."

But what if there was support for us? What if, there was Someone always available and accessible that could meet our need, fill the gap where others have failed?

122

Tools

And what if that person was God? You don't have to be religious to access God. You just need to seek Him. If you seek Him, you will find him.

How do we find God?

We go back to the beginning.

Robert Coles, a leading researcher in the field of children did a research project where he interviewed children from around the world, from many faith backgrounds (meaning, their parents belonged to a particular faith group such as Jewish, Muslim, or Christian.) But he also interviewed children whose parents identified as Atheist. (no belief in God) The children he interviewed were young enough not to have been greatly influenced.

What he found was that every child he interviewed believed in God. Every child described God as a person – with a face that smiled and frowned. The majority of them believed God was sad when they were bad and happy when they were good and many of them went on to describe a very deep and close relationship that they had with God – despite having had no teaching about Him. They talked to Him and about Him.

This amazed Dr. Coles because the evidence suggested that the children's beliefs seemed to be intuitive rather than learned. God seems to be part of all of our beginnings.

But then many of us dismissed him.

Maybe like you did.

Why? Perhaps we followed our Parent's example. Perhaps our community or cultural group had no talk of Him. Perhaps because someone's bad experiences with religion soured us to Him.

123

Geri Holmes

Or perhaps we dismissed him because we blamed him for not intervening in tragic circumstances.

But what if the messages we got about Him were misleading – and we were actually quite right to begin our life believing?

Can we turn back and return to Him again?

That means he is not a higher power, a force of nature or nature itself, but a person who speaks, who thinks, who acts and who relates to us. He is another Person who is always present. He relates to children. He relates to adults.

And as He was in childhood so is He now; He is watchful and aware.

And He is Love.

He embodies love and loves us. Just as we love our child, He loves us and understands more than most what motivates us or drives us. He knows our inner desires, needs and hopes. And he cares.

We could return to Him...

Or, we could continue to dismiss Him.

God is the source of Comfort

One of the most significant roles a parent plays in the life of a young child is to embrace them, soothe them and comfort them. Do you remember those times? Perhaps you had a nightmare and without much thought ran to your parent's room or screamed for Mommy.

Tools

They may have allowed you to crawl in beside them. Or they went back to your bed and tucked you in, reassured you, said soothing words such as "It's okay, you're ok. You're safe now." It helped. It worked.

Comfort. We needed it then. We still need it now.

It's one of the things we hope to gain in our marriage. Our heart cries out, "Will you comfort me, hold me, protect me, reassure me?"

And then they fail us. They may even be the source of our discomfort.

But the need to be comforted cannot be denied. We remain vulnerable and many times we lack the tools to comfort ourselves.

We may reach out for our friends or family. But they are not always there for us. We are alone.

But God, who loves us, understands us and is without judgment (contrary to some people's ideas) and is always present can and will comfort us.

You may ask, "Why hasn't He done it then?"

Because he is a Gentleman! He stands at the door and knocks. He waits. He came running at the first moment of your distress; at the first sign of your loneliness.

And He waits.

God is not to blame

Of course if we have experienced pain and hurt and we have blamed God it is difficult to ask for Him to show himself. Many people are angry at God because they believe if God indeed is all powerful and

125

Geri Holmes

almighty, he should have stopped what was happening to them or the ones they love. Or perhaps He should have stopped famine, poverty or war. He should not have allowed it.

However, what if instead of blaming him we understood that he was present and that he understood the heart of all parties involved? What if we understood that he wept with us, grieved with us, and stood with hands tied – that He was powerless because of the limits he chose to put on himself?

Limits? What limits?

Free will is the part that makes us human. Our ability to choose for ourselves gives us the dignity of personhood. For God to interfere – to "control" the abuser, or the murderer– would be to interfere with our core identity. We would be puppets instead of people.

If you are a parent you understand this right to choose. You have experienced the anger and the rage you feel when your child chooses badly and affects others by his/her poor choice. And yet like God, you cannot control, force or "make" your child obey; you can only watch with sorrow and at times helplessness. You may discipline the behavior hoping that after they experience the consequences of their action, they will choose better the next time. But ultimately, we have no control. They must choose.

In the same way, God is a parent.

He is present in our lives but waiting: waiting for you to ask Him so he could engage with you. He waits for your permission. He is respectful. Even now.

So what does this have to do with marriage?

Tools

When you are needing more, wanting more, and emotionally reaching for more and you dismiss God by blaming Him, you may be cutting off a Divine Source that would help you get the help you need.

I have come to experience God as my husband many times in my life –whether I was in the marriage or not. He has comforted me and met emotional needs that my husband either chose not to meet or did not have the capacity to do so.

My husband failed me in so many ways. But I stayed – because again and again when I turned to God he helped me.

Do you have to stay?

There are no "have tos" with God. Whether you stay or you leave He is with you. He is present.

But sometimes when you find your help in God, you don't need to leave.

And that leads me to my next point.

God is your Champion

God believes in you more than anyone.

I have never met anyone who did not struggle at one level or another with their self-worth. Because of our struggle our spousal relationship becomes very important to us: we often expect the one that loves us to foster and build us up. We assume they will believe in us.

It is unfortunate but a spouse can be the most discouraging and hurtful person in our life.

127

Geri Holmes

One of the most devastating things about domestic violence or living with abuse of any kind is that it strips the person of their worth and value. An abuser may cause their partner to feel useless, ignorant and incapable of trusting herself. (And never would I counsel a person to stay in that situation).

But criticism and nasty fights in a "normal" marriage can have the same devastating results. The shaming and judging can deeply affect a woman. Any woman. Every marriage will have those moments in them. People lose it, say things they shouldn't and the mouth can be the cruelest weapon of all.

So how do we recover?

We need to recapture the Truth. We need to be reminded about who we really are. We are worthy. We are acceptable. We are loveable. We are wanted. We are good enough. (And not because another man wants us!)

How do we know?

Because the One who made us, who was instrumental in forming us in our mother's womb, cannot make junk! It did not matter the conditions in which we were conceived, or whether the parents that conceived us continued to love us.

God wanted us.

He did then and He does now.

When we acknowledge God as present in our marriage we can run to Him to align ourselves with the Truth. We can reject the hurtful things someone has said– whether in our childhood or in our marriage – and we can re-orient ourselves to the Truth of who we are.

Tools

We matter.

How do we know we matter?

Because God says so.

Your DNA declares your uniqueness – your specialness and your value. You are singularly important to God.

God has paid your debt

Earlier in the book we spoke of forgiveness and the humility we need to ask for it and to offer it to others who have wronged us. Sometimes it is really hard to leave the past behind. Most of us believe that all "bad" behavior should be punished, or at least consequenced in some way. This makes sense to us. It is how we raise our children and teach them to choose what is good.

But in adult relationships this is a problem. How long should we punish others? How long should we punish ourselves for mistakes and failures? We have need for absolution – for a clean page.

And this may be why you may want to leave your marriage.

- You may want a clean page with no bad memories.
  Sometimes we can't imagine living a life that has all the memories of hurt and betrayal or pain written on the pages. We want to be free of past hurt and pain.

- You may want freedom from the feelings of failure or shame. When a marriage is difficult we tend to own it. So starting fresh means we won't wake up every morning with this feeling of helplessness or powerlessness and the worry that we might be the problem.

129

Geri Holmes

- You may want a fresh start.
  Turning a new leaf can make us feel hopeful that we can have a new beginning.

The sad thing about leaving a marriage in order to find another fresh start is that it won't be long before marks appear again. No, we may not make the same mistakes again but I am confident we will make others.

And so will he.

He may be a different man but he will be a human one. He may not betray you but he will at some other level disappoint you.

Remember the dartboard. We have all missed the mark.

So what do we do with a marked up life, scarred by disappointment and betrayal or marked by our own failures and mess-ups?

We give it to God.

God has the power to clean a page

He has the power to offer forgiveness when we cannot forgive ourselves. He has the power to help us "forget" and move on with hope and optimism.

Through Him we do not have to carry the regret and the life-time sentence of repayment. We do not need to prove to anyone that we are different or better because forgiveness is so complete it is as if it never happened.

How do we know?

Tools

The whole story of God is that being "personal" he needed to relate to us, and us to him. So he made a way of presenting himself that is more relatable. He sent his Son Jesus to live on planet earth in human skin, facing human challenges and human pain so he could first and foremost identify with us. It can never be said, 'God doesn't get what I am feeling.' He most certainly does.

Second, God made a payment for every one of our mess-ups. He made a way of paying off the debts we owe others so we don't have to keep paying. Although Jesus Christ had done nothing wrong he was judged, and sentenced to death – and he went there gladly. Why? To free you of your need to pay off your debt! You do not need to prove your worthiness again. He paid it for you by his death on a cross. He paid for your mistakes with his own life.

The ability to relate to God is so simple the child can understand. In fact, it is our adult independence and prideful determination to make life work on our own that cuts us off from the greatest Resource we have to cope with the difficulties of life and marriage.

When we dismiss God we reject his offer of comfort.

When we dismiss God we reject his affirmation of us as his child. We reject His delight in us and His reassurance of our great worth and value.

Finally when we dismiss God we reject his offer of pardon and of forgiveness and the opportunity to look forward with hope and joy knowing he has cleaned the slate, and offered us a new page.

Need a repair in your marriage?

Go back to the beginning and find God again. Seek Him out among those who clearly demonstrate their dependence on Him. Open the door and let Him in. Reconnect.

OWN it.

1. Consider your early childhood. Can you remember believing in God? When did it change? Why did it change?

2. What blockades or barriers stand in the way of you having a relationship with God? Have you ever thought about forgiving God?

3. If you want to engage with God but don't know how to begin, find a place in nature where you feel the closest to him and pray this prayer,

Dear God. I don't know you but I want to. I am here seeking for you. Will you open my eyes to see you, open my ears to hear you, open my heart to receive you? And God, I understand I have sinned or made many mistakes, so would you forgive me? Would you clean my page? I give it to you. I am willing to forgive others with your help. I am willing to pursue a relationship with you. Here I am.

Final Thoughts

I struggled to write this book because I was concerned it would come off negative. Perhaps you felt bad as you read chapter after chapter confronting some habit or attitude that may affect your marriage in negative ways.

But know this. I believe in you, and the tremendous power you have as a woman to set the tone for a great relationship. I believe women are great influencers.

And men love women!!!

Since I began counseling the numbers of men I see daily have grown. Sometimes in any given week I see more men than women. I am struck by their desperation to fix their marriage. They are devastated when their wives leave. They are motivated to change. They care.

By listening carefully and by watching how men and women interact in the counseling office I began to see familiar patterns. As I mentioned in the introduction – I found myself repeating certain ideas again and again. Men would listen as I instructed women and go completely silent. It was as if they dared not nod or show agreement.

But I saw relief on their faces.

Why? Because at least for a moment they understood they are not the only problem.

Geri Holmes

A healthy marriage is made of two healthy people. It's hard to be healthy if we are caught up in blame. We cannot control what another person does – we may not like his dance moves or his missteps. But as one person said, if only one person takes dancing lessons, we will never dance the same again.

I want to encourage you to reflect on the chapters as sincerely as you are able. Allow yourself to go through the angst of self-discovery. Is there anything here that you can work on? Is there anything here you can own?

Then do it. Try it. Swallow your pride and work on it.

Your marriage will change because you will.

And perhaps it won't need to end at all.

End Notes: For further study

Chapter 1

Bloom, Linda & Charlie, *The Real Reason that Opposites Attract*, Psychology Today, August 2014, https://www.psychologytoday.com/blog/stronger-the-broken-places/201401/the-real-reason-opposites-attract

Nield, David, *Scientists Have Found Genetic Links Between Personality Traits And Psychiatric Diseases* Science Alert, December 2016, https://www.sciencealert.com/scientists-find-genetic-links-between-personality-traits-and-psychiatric-diseases

Clear, James, How Long Does it Actually Take to Form a New Habit? (Backed by Science) https://jamesclear.com/new-habit

An article summarizing oxytocin: https://www.medicalnewstoday.com/articles/275795.php

Research: The release of oxytocin in the man's brain during intercourse https://joe.bioscientifica.com/view/journals/joe/107/1/joe_107_1_013.xml and https://www.ncbi.nlm.nih.gov/pmc/articles/PMC3936960/

The role of oxytocin in bonding couples/social behavior

https://nyaspubs.onlinelibrary.wiley.com/doi/abs/10.1111/j.1749-6632.1992.tb34356.x

Geri Holmes

Pair-bonding, romantic love and hormones

https://journals.sagepub.com/doi/abs/10.1177/1745691614561683

I might also mention that oxytocin plays a role in keeping a man faithful. Studies have shown that men in monogamous relationships who were given oxytocin nasal spray more frequently distanced themselves from women who were not their wife! https://www.theatlantic.com/health/archive/2012/11/study-oxytocin-the-love-hormone-makes-men-in-relationships-want-to-stay-away-from-other-women/265314/

Chapter 2

Gungor, Mark, *Laugh Your Way to a Better Marriage: Unlocking the* Secrets to Life, Love and Marriage, Atria Books, March 2008

Cecile Borkhataria *The REAL difference between men and women: Researchers find 6,500 genes differ between the sexes,* Daily Mail.com, May 2017. http://www.dailymail.co.uk/sciencetech/article-4475252/There-6-500-genetic-differences-men-women.html

Tuck C Ngun, Negar Ghahramani, Francisco J. Sánchez, Sven Bocklandt, and Eric Vilain, *The Genetics of Sex Differences in Brain and Behavior,* PMC, April 2011. https://www.ncbi.nlm.nih.gov/pmc/articles/PMC3030621

Rupp, Heather and Kim Wallen. Sex Differences in Response to Visual Sexual Stimuli: A Review PMC, August 2017 https://www.ncbi.nlm.nih.gov/pmc/articles/PMC2739403

https://www.sciencedirect.com/topics/medicine-and-dentistry/behavioral-endocrinology

Tools

Chapter Four

Law Nolte, Dorothy, *Children Learn What They Live* (poem) Thomas Allen & Son Ltd, 1972

CPSIA information can be obtained
at www.ICGtesting.com
Printed in the USA
BVHW071910201220
595727BV00001B/2